Cambridge Primary Path

Foundation

Activity Book

Martha Fernández

1 Who am I?

1 ▶ 1.1 **Watch the video. Match to complete the graphic organizer.**

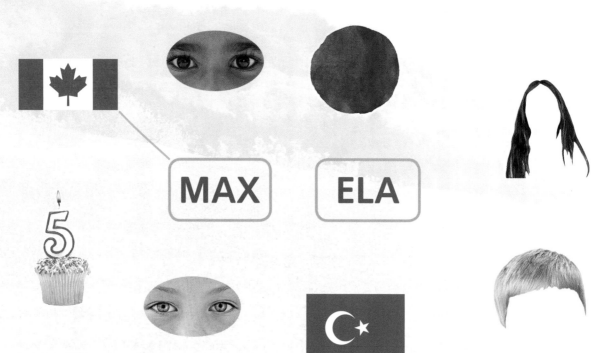

MAX   ELA

2 Key Words 1 **Circle.**

a **girl**

b **hair**

c **boy**

d **brown**

1 Key Words 2 **Trace.**

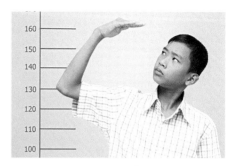

l o n g   c u r l y   t a l l

s t r a i g h t   b l o n d

2 **Match the opposites.**

blond

long

curly

short

straight

brown

Reading Strategy: Similarities and Differences

1 **What's similar? Circle.**

2 **Read** with your teacher's help. **What's similar? What's different?**

This Is My Class!

Ula is tall.
Paul is short.

Ula is a girl.
Maya is a girl.

Maya is a girl.
Ben is a boy.

Ben   Maya   Paul   Ula

③ Match.

Ben

Paul

Maya

Ula

straight hair

blond hair

curly hair

red hair

④ Trace.

Ben
Paul

Ula
Maya

Ben
Paul

Ula
Maya

⑤ Color.

1

2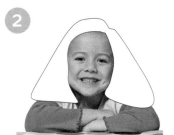

3

4

a Ula has red hair.

b Maya has blond hair.

c Ben has curly brown hair.

d Paul has straight brown hair.

Verb *to be*: am, is

I am **short.**
He is **six years old.**
She is **tall.**

I'm not **tall.**
He's not **five years old.**
She's not **short.**

1 Circle *am* and *is*. Color.

a I'm not tall.

b She is six years old.

c I am five years old.

d He's not short.

2 Circle *am* or *is*.

a I **am** / **is** tall.

b She **am** / **is** tall.

3 Trace. Match.

a She **is** Anna.

b I **'m not** five years old.

c He **is** Emir.

1

2

3

6

(4) Match.

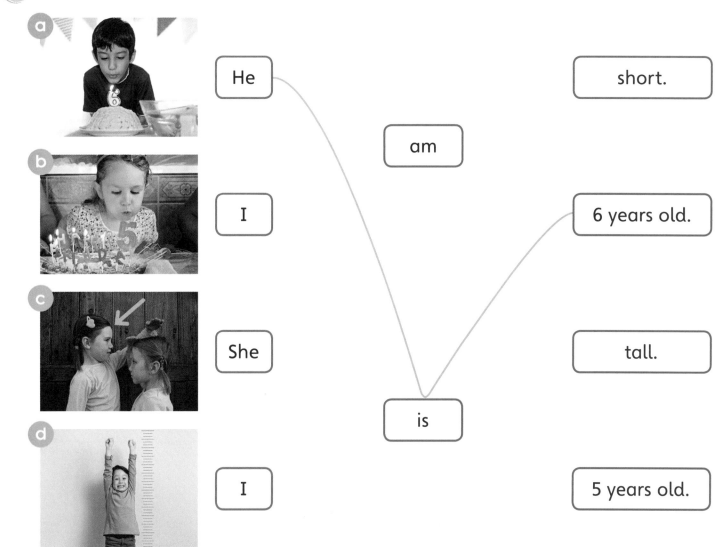

a

He

am

short.

b

I

6 years old.

c

She

tall.

is

d

I

5 years old.

My Life

Answer. Draw.

My name is _____.

I am  years old.   My favorite color is  .

I am **tall / short.**

1 Trace.

The Alphabet Song

A B C D E F G H I
J K L M N O P Q R
S T U V W X Y Z

2 Color.

E A I P T X M

A B C D E F G H I J K L M
N O P Q R S T U V W X Y Z

Oracy

1 Trace. Match.

Listen.

Share.

Ask.

Do you understand?

Capital and Lowercase Letters

This is a capital letter: A   This is a lowercase letter: a

(1) Mark ✓ the capital letters.

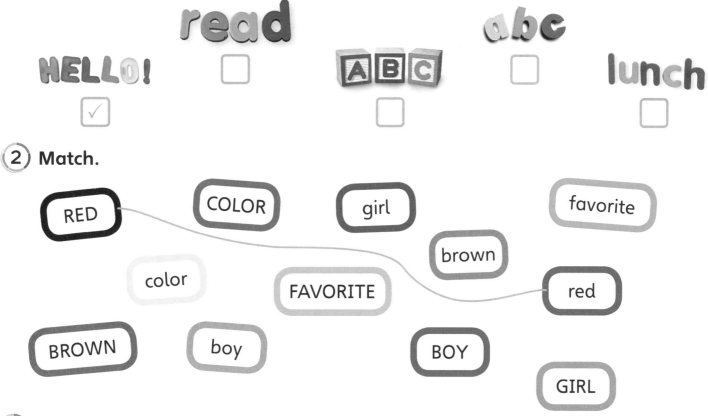

read ☐

HELLO! ☑

ABC ☐

abc ☐

lunch ☐

(2) Match.

RED   COLOR   girl   favorite

brown

color   FAVORITE   red

BROWN   boy   BOY

GIRL

(3) Circle or underline.

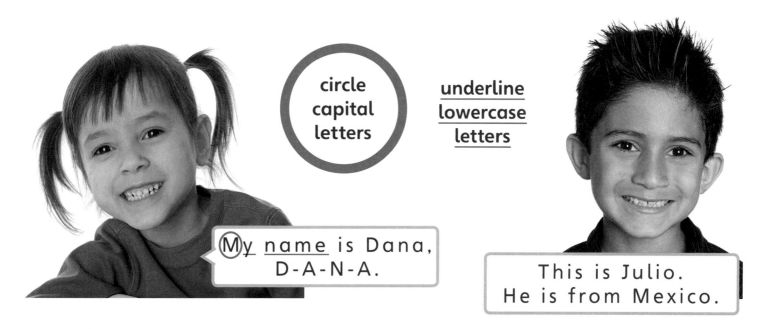

circle capital letters

underline lowercase letters

(M)y name is Dana, D-A-N-A.

This is Julio. He is from Mexico.

1 Trace.

This is Selda.

He's Lee.

I'm Ana

My name is Ken.

2 Color. Trace.

5 FIVE   **6 SIX**

I'm $five$ years old.

I'm six years old.

Ready to Read: Fiction

1 **Key Words 4** Circle.

a

old / young

b

fast / slow

c

fast / slow

d

tired / happy

2 Match.

1

2

3

5

4

a She is tired.

b They are happy.

c I am fast.

d He is slow.

e He is old.

11

Reading Strategy: Real or Fantasy?

1 **Circle.**

 real  fantasy

2 **Read** with your teacher's help.

The Rabbit and the Turtle

She's old. He's young. They are happy.

She's slow. He's fast.

Explore the Text

1B

(3) **Match.**

3

2

1

4

(4) **Circle.**

a

is fast.

b

is slow.

c

is tired.

d

is number 1.

e

is happy.

13

Grammar in Context

Verb *to be*: *are*

He is young.   **He isn't old.**
You are happy.   **You aren't sad.**

1 **Look. Match.**

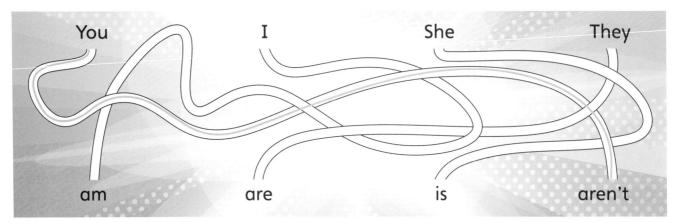

You   I   She   They

am   are   is   aren't

2 **Match. Circle *are* and *aren't*.**

a   They (are) fast.
b   You are young
c   You aren't happy.

3 **Circle.**

You (are) / is happy.

I **is / am** tired.

They **are / is** tall.

You **are / aren't** old.

She **is / isn't** fast.

14

4 Match. Trace *am*, *is*, and *are*.

a You **are** young. Grandpa **is** old.

b He **is** fast. I **am** slow.

c They **are** tall. You **are** short.

5 Match and color.

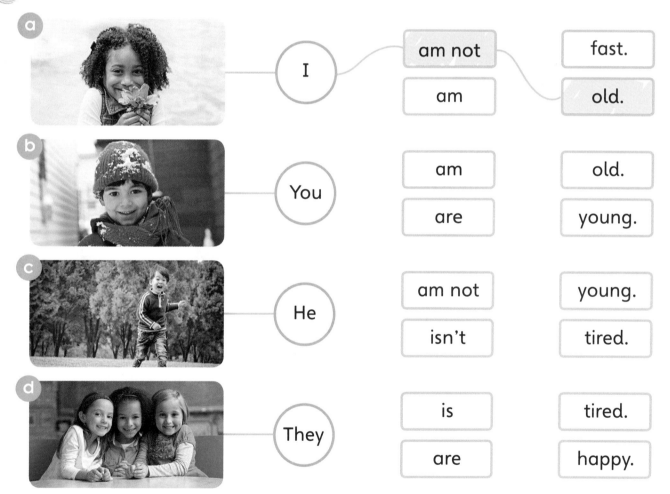

am not	fast.
am	old.

I

am	old.
are	young.

You

am not	young.
isn't	tired.

He

is	tired.
are	happy.

They

My Life

Mark √ facts about yourself.

I'm happy. ☐   I'm tall. ☐   I'm young. ☐   I'm old. ☐

1 **Mark the children who are different ✓ with your teacher's help.**

a

b
 ✓

c

d

2 **Match.**

a He's a boy. He has short brown hair.

b She's a girl. She has straight blond hair.

c He's a boy. He has short blond hair.

d She's a girl. She has curly brown hair.

1

2

3

4

3 **Draw yourself and a friend.**

 Are you similar? Are you different?

The Big Challenge and Oracy

How can we talk about ourselves?

Answer with your teacher's help.

Color or .

1 I made a collage. **or**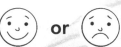

2 I described myself. 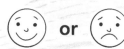 **or**

3 I talked about my favorite things. **or**

Oracy

Check Your Oracy!

1 I listened to others.	**Yes / No**	
2 I took turns.	**Yes / No**	
3 I shared my ideas.	**Yes / No**	

Follow the ground rules!

1 Circle.

a boy girl

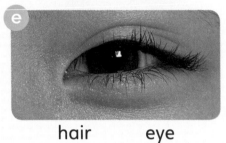

b hair eye

c boy girl

d brown red

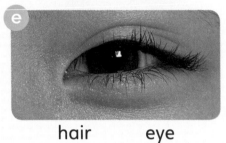

e hair eye

f young old

2 Mark ✓.

a She has short hair.
She has long hair. ☐

b I have curly hair. ☐
I have straight hair. ☐

c He is tired. ☐
He is fast. ☐

d You have blond hair. ☐
You have brown hair. ☐

3 Trace.

Ken is t a l l.

Liz is s h o r t.

They are d i f f e r e n t.

4 **Circle *am* or *is*.**

a I (am) / is a boy. She **are** / **is** a girl.

b She **is** / **are** tall. I **am** / **is** short.

c I **am** / **is** fast. She **am** / **is** slow.

d She **am** / **is** happy. I **am** / **is** happy, too!

5 **Match.**

a I

b You

c He

d She

are my friend.

is short.

is tall.

am happy.

6 **Trace.**

t h a n k   y o u

s t o p

SPEAKING MISSION

1 Circle.

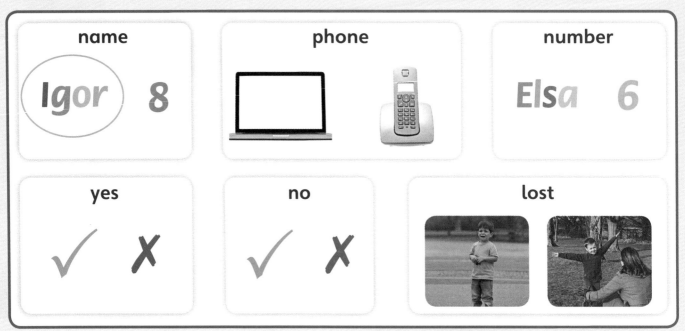

name	phone	number
(Igor) 8		Elsa 6

yes	no	lost
✓ X	✓ X	

2 Match.

a What's your name? —————— I'm 6.

b How old are you? —————— Abu Naser.

c What's your phone number? 5566-7823.

3 Number 1, 2, 3.

1 What's your name?

2 How old are you?

3 Are you lost?

_____ No, I'm not lost.

_1_ My name is Igor.

_____ I am 6.

What can you remember about ... Unit 1?

1 Circle.

She has **short / long** hair.

2 Match.

I	is tall.
He	are fast.
You	am tired.

3 Circle the brown crayon.

4 Match the opposites.

fast	young
long	slow
old	short

5 Match.

B   c   b   g

6 Trace.

M m O o P p

Check your answers in the Student's Book. How did you do?
5–6 ☐ Great!   3–4 ☐ Good!   0–2 ☐ Try harder!

? 😀 Who am I?

My name is _____.

I am _____ years old.

2 What is school?

1 ▶ 2.1 **Watch the video. Circle to complete the graphic organizer.**

classroom

teacher

playground

School

2 Key Words 1 **Match.**

desk

teacher

classroom

gym

bathroom

playground

22

1 Key Words 2 **Circle.**

library

schoolbag

pencil case

notebook

colored pencil

eraser

2 **Match. Color.**

notebook eraser schoolbag pencil case

Reading Strategy: Classifying

(1) **What is at school? Circle.**

(2) **Read** with your teacher's help.

My Classroom

The pencil is blue.

The pencil case is purple.

The notebook is red.

The chair is purple.

The schoolbag is blue.

The apple is green.

(3) **Read the text again. Circle.**

pencil

apple

chair

(4) **Match.**

notebook

pencil case

schoolbag

(5) **Circle. Color.**

blue chair

red apple

green pencil

Articles: *a, an*

| a **desk** | an **eraser** |
| a **pencil** | an **apple** |

**(1) Circle *a* and *an*.
Match.**

a It's (a) chair.

b It's an eraser.

c It's a pencil case.

d It's an apple.

(2) Trace. Mark ✓.

a **an** eraser

 ✓

 ☐

b **a** notebook

 ☐

 ☐

c apples

 ☐

 ☐

d **a** desk

 ☐

 ☐

e **an** orange

 ☐

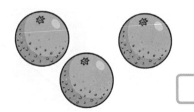 ☐

26

③ Trace. Draw.

a notebook

a schoolbag

an orange

④ Circle *a* or *an*.

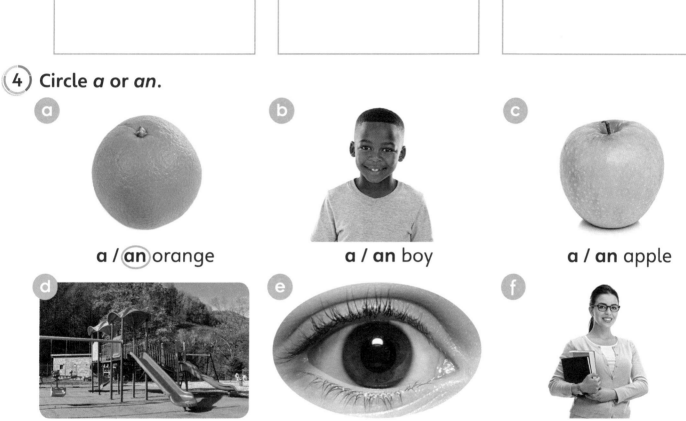

a a / (an) orange

b a / an boy

c a / an apple

d a / an playground

e a / an eye

f a / an teacher

My Life

Mark ✓.

What's in your school?

1 Say. Color.

(c) (b)

car

10 (t) (n)

ten

(p) (n)

pen

(p) (n)

net

(h) (t)

hat

(b) (h)

boy

2 Match. Trace.

a ten ——————
b Car
c boy
d hat
e nine

Cat
toy
net
big
hello

1 Do you agree? Circle or .

a Puzzles are great!

b Books are fun!

Alphabetical Order

A B C D E F G H I J K L M N O P Q R S T U V W X Y Z
a b c d e f g h i j k l m n o p q r s t u v w x y z

(1) Color in order.

a b w **c** r **d** e f z g x h i j y k l z m
n o b p q r s a t u v f w x y b z

(2) Circle.

a	(ant)	pencil	(apple)
b	car	fish	cat
c	eight	eraser	desk
d	hat	chair	hen

(1) Put in alphabetical order.

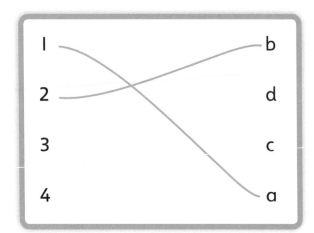

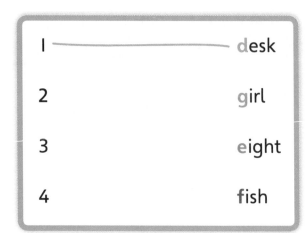

(2) Trace. Match.

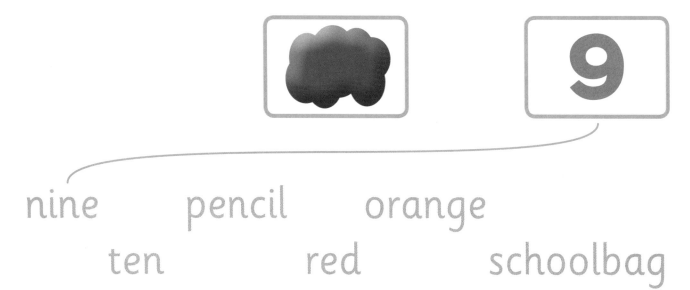

nine   pencil   orange

ten   red   schoolbag

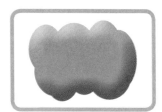

(3) Write.

My name is _____.

1 Key Words 4 **Color.**

a

story   lunchbox

b

sad   hungry

c

story   lunchbox

d

sad   mad

e

surprised   sad

f

sad   mad

2 **Match.**

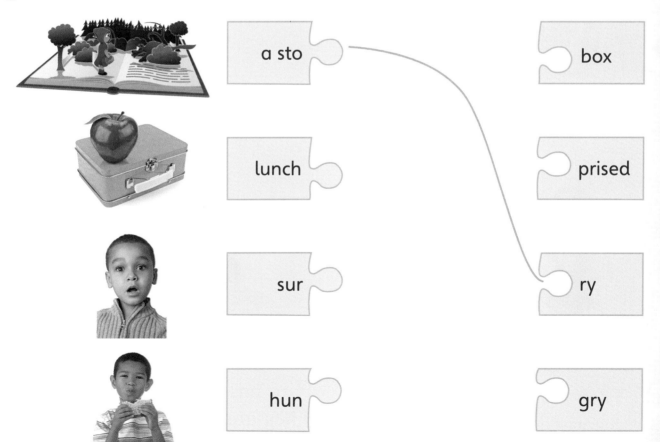

a sto ——— ry

lunch   box

sur   prised

hun   gry

Reading Strategy: Understanding a Character's Feelings

① **Look. Circle.**

sad   happy

It's my lunchbox!

This is not my lunchbox.

School is fun!

I can't find my classmates!

② **Read** with your teacher's help.

Ada's Birthday at School

It's Ada's birthday. She is six today. She is in school.

Thank you!

Ada and Hira are on the playground. Hira has a present for Ada.

Look. They are colored pencils! Ada is surprised.

Ada has a colored pencil. Hira has a colored pencil. They are happy.

(3) **Match.**

This is

This is

Hira .

Ada is

6 .

Ada has a

Hira has a

Ada .

(4) **Circle.**

tired (hungry)

mad   surprised

happy   sad

(5) **Trace.**

h a p p y   s u r p r i s e d   h u n g r y

Possessive Pronouns: *my, your, his, her*

 This is my pencil.

 This is your eraser.

 This is his lunchbox.

 This is her schoolbag.

1) Match.

| My pencil is green. | Her pencil is red. | His pencil is blue. | Your pencil is green. |

2) Circle.

my / your
classroom

my / your
lunchbox

his / her
notebook

his / her
schoolbag

3 **Color.**

a My book is .

b His book is .

c Her book is .

4 **Trace.**

This is
her present.

This is
his book.

This is
my desk.

This is
your chair.

My Life

Draw. Color.

My schoolbag is .   My pencil case is .   My notebook is .

Values: Taking Care of Your School Objects

1 Circle 😊 or 🙁 .

 😊 🙁

 😊 🙁

 😊 🙁

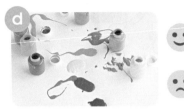 😊 🙁

 😊 🙁

 😊 🙁

2 Mark ✓ .

I take care of
my school objects.

3 Draw yourself in school.

I take care of
my school objects.

The Big Challenge

How can we make a classroom map?

Answer with your teacher's help.

Color 😊 or 🙁 .

1 I made a classroom map.   😊 or 🙁

2 I named things in my classroom.   😊 or 🙁

3 I talked about classroom objects.   😊 or 🙁

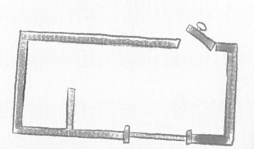

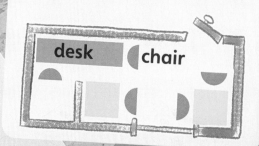
desk   chair

Oracy

Check Your Oracy!	
1 I listened to my teacher.	Yes / No
2 I said *Yes* when I agreed.	Yes / No
3 I said *No* when I disagreed.	Yes / No

Yes!

1 Circle.

a (classroom)　　　　b gym　　　c library　　　d playground

　bathroom　　　　　　　bathroom　　　gym　　　　　classroom

2 Color.

desk 　　notebook 　　lunchbox

eraser 　　pencil case 　　colored pencil

3 Trace.

a classmates　　b apple

c sad　　　　　　d story

e teacher　　　　f mad

4 **Match.**

a   an

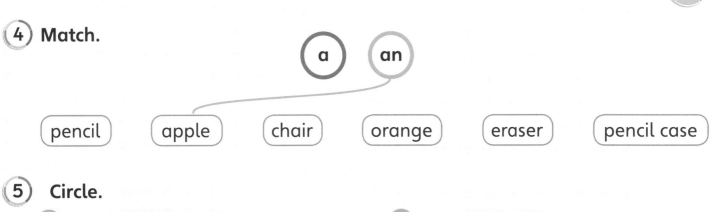

pencil   apple   chair   orange   eraser   pencil case

5 **Circle.**

a

This is my / his schoolbag.

b

This is her / his pencil.

c

This is her / his notebook.

d

This is his / your lunchbox.

6 **Put in alphabetical order.**

1 _____ eraser

2 _____ library

3 _____ bathroom

4 _____ apple

5 _____ playground

SPEAKING MISSION

1 Match.

scissors

crayons

ruler

pencil sharpener

marker

glue

2 Circle.

a   Can I borrow your ?   （marker）/ scissors

b   I don't have a 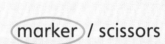 .   ruler / crayon

c   Can I borrow your ?   marker / crayon

d   I don't have a  .   pencil sharpener / notebook

3 Number 1, 2, and 3.

<u>1</u> Can I borrow your ruler?

____ Sorry! I don't have a ruler.

____ No problem!

<u>1</u> Can I borrow your crayon?

____ Sure. Here you are!

____ Thank you!

Wrap-up

2

What can you remember about ... Unit 2?

1 Circle.

This is the **library / gym**.

2 Match.

a   orange

an   desk

3 Match.

hat   cat

library   hello

car   long

4 Trace.

a g b t   a b c d

5 Circle.

Max can't find **his / her** school things. He is **mad / happy**.

6 Circle the ruler.

Check your answers in the Student's Book. How did you do?

5–6 ☐ **Great!**   3–4 ☐ **Good!**   0–2 ☐ **Try harder!**

? 😊 What is school?

Circle.

What is a toy?

1 ▶ 3.1 **Watch the video. Draw lines to the toys in the graphic organizer.**

Toys

2 Key Words 1 **Circle.**

(toy)   box

tablet   airplane

house   gym

box   tablet

toy   box

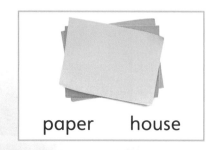

paper   house

Unit 3A **Ready to Read:** Nonfiction

 3A

1 Key Words 2 **Match.**

dollhouse   tent   robot   jump rope   train   fun

2 **Color. Count. Write the number.**

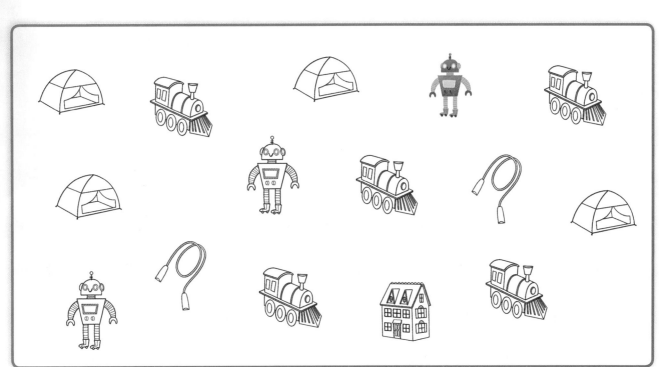

____ dollhouse   _3_ robots   ____ jump ropes   ____ trains   ____ tents

Reading Strategy: Classifying Words

1 **Circle in the correct color.**

 toys

 names

 colors

Lucas

white

Emma

black

jump rope

train

2 **Read** with your teacher's help. **Circle the colors.**

Toys

Rob has a red and brown house.

Ayaz has a red car.

Lisa has a blue and white airplane.

Ian has a blue, green, and black train.

Irina has a green jump rope.

3 Read the text again. Match.

a Rob

b Ayaz

c Lisa

d Ian

e Irina

4 Circle.

names	Ayaz	Rob	red	Lisa	car

toys	green	train	red	airplane	jump rope

colors	blue	Rab	brown	house	green

5 Match.

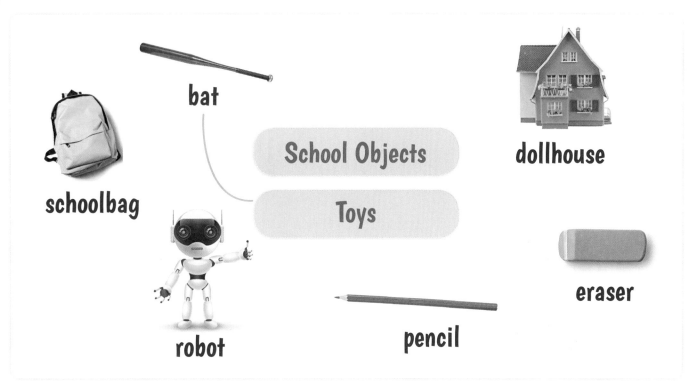

bat

schoolbag

robot

School Objects

Toys

dollhouse

pencil

eraser

Commands

| March! |  | Listen! |  | Stand! |  |
| Sit! |  | Stop! |  | Jump! |  |

1 Match.

a Look!

b March!

c Run!

d Listen!

e Jump!

2 Circle.

a  Sit! **Jump!**

b  Stop! Sit!

c  Stand! Run!

d  Run! Sit!

46

3 Trace.

Stop!

Run!

Listen!

4 Color the commands.

Stand!   Sit!   Yes.   Thank you.   Stop!   I'm Emma.

My Life

Draw yourself.

March!   Sit!   Run!

Phonics

1 Say. Color. Match. en at

cat

ten

hen

bat

pen

hat

2 Say. Cross out ✗ the different sound.

a ten pen ~~bat~~

b hen hat pen

c cat ten bat

d ten pen hat

e hen cat pen

Oracy

1 Who is listening actively? Mark ✓.

48

3A

Complete Sentences

| This is a sentence: | The toys are big. |
| This is a not a sentence: | the toys |

1 Trace.

a **R**ania is a girl.

b **S**he has a toy.

c **T**he toy is yellow.

d **I**t's a robot.

2 Circle.

This is a sentence.   not a sentence

a (I have an airplane.)

b (brown eyes)

c the yellow train

d an orange car

e I have a toy box.

f two blue pencils

g Aiko has black hair.

My name is Aiko.

49

1 Match.

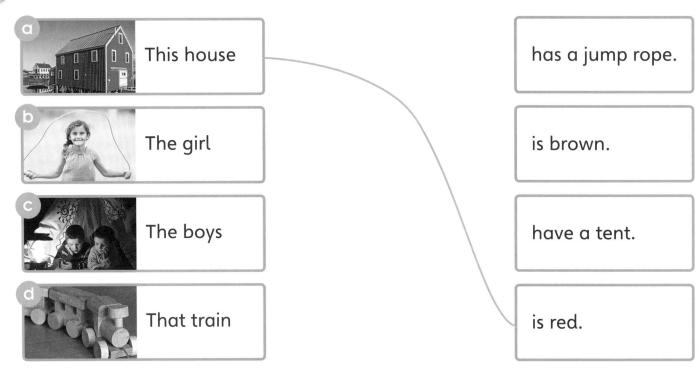

a | This house
b | The girl
c | The boys
d | That train

has a jump rope.

is brown.

have a tent.

is red.

2 Color.

She has | a tablet.
| a house.

It's | a tent.
| an airplane.

This is | a schoolbag.
| a box.

Ready to Read: Fiction

1 Key Words 4 **Circle.**

a
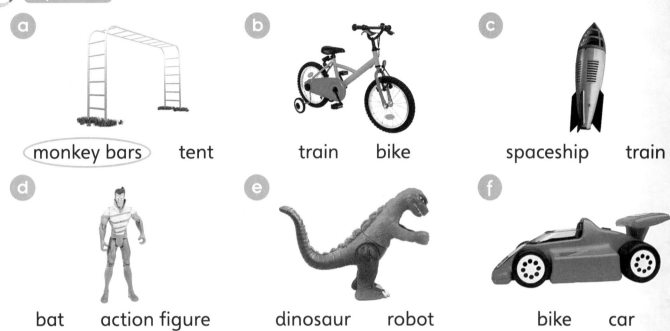
(monkey bars)   tent

b   train   bike

c   spaceship   train

d   bat   action figure

e   dinosaur   robot

f   bike   car

2 **Color.**

a The monkey bars are red.

b The bike is yellow.

c The car is blue.

d The action figure is brown.

e The dinosaur is green.

f The spaceship is orange.

Reading Strategy: Ordering Story Events

1. **Number 1, 2, and 3.**

2. **Read** with your teacher's help. **Circle the commands.**

The Toy Box

Look!

It's a toy box!

Look! It's an action figure.

I have a robot!

Look! I see a spaceship!

I see a dinosaur! Run!

Monkey bars are fun! Jump!

3 Number 1, 2, and 3.

4 Circle the correct command.

It's a toy box!   Monkey bars are fun!   I see a dinosaur!

Run! (Look!)   Jump!   Stop!   Sit!   Run!

5 Trace. Draw an action figure.

Jump!   Run!

Negative Commands

Don't sit!    Don't jump!

1 **Circle the negative commands.**

a (Don't stop!)   b Jump!   c Sit!

d Don't stand!   e March!   f Don't run!

2 **Match.**

a Don't run!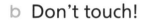

b Don't touch!

c Don't sit!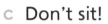

d Don't jump!

3 **Circle.**

Sit!   (Don't sit!)   Stop!   Don't stop!   Touch!   Don't touch!

SB page 67

(4) Mark ✓.

a Don't jump!

b Don't play!

c Don't talk!

d Don't run!

(5) Trace.

a Don't run!   b Don't talk!   c Don't sit!

My Life

Draw yourself.

Listen!   Don't touch!

1 Who is sharing? Mark ✓.

 a ✓

 b

 c

 d

 e

 f

2 Circle what we share.

3 Draw yourself.

What do you share with a friend?

The Big Challenge and Oracy

How can we make a toy?

Answer with your teacher's help.

Color **or** .

1 I made a toy. **or**

2 I talked about toys. **or**

3 I told the class about my toy. 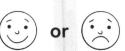 **or**

Oracy

Check Your Oracy!

1 Did you listen actively to your classmates?	Yes / No
2 Did you say *Please repeat that?*	Yes / No

Do you like (action figures)?

1 **Color.**

a monkey bars   b box

c dinosaur   d robot

2 **Match.**

house   train   spaceship   car   airplane

3 **Trace.**

a They are c h i l d r e n.

b The girl has a s p a c e s h i p.

c The boy has a b i k e.

d They have f u n.

(4) **Match.**

Stop!

Run!

Look!

Jump!

Listen!

(5) **Trace.**

Run!

Don't march!

Sit!

Don't jump!

(6) **Color the sentences.**

a The girl has a robot.

b the boy

c That's a toy box.

d I have a dinosaur.

e are blue

① **Match.**

board game

play dough

boat

dinosaur

soccer ball

② **Trace. Circle.**

a This is a

(jigsaw puzzle.)

board game.

b Let's buy a

robot.

doll.

③ **Number I, 2 and 3.**

_1_ A jump rope, please!

____ Here you go!

____ Thank you!

60

What can you remember about ... Unit 3?

1 **Match.**

bike

monkey bars

spaceship

2 **Circle.**

This **airplane / boat** is red.

3 **Circle blue or green.**

cat   hen

hat   pen   ten   bat

4 **Circle.**

Hiro and **Ela / Olivia** are friends.

5 **Match.**

Run!

Don't jump!

6 **Circle the sentence.**

the toy   The toy is yellow.

Check your answers in the Student's Book. How did you do?
5–6 ☐ **Great!** 3–4 ☐ **Good!** 0–2 ☐ **Try harder!**

? 😊 **What is a toy?**

Color.

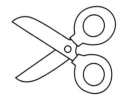

4   What makes a home?

1 ▶ 4.1   **Watch the video. What do you do at home? Draw to complete the graphic organizer.**

bedroom

dining room

Home

living room

kitchen

2 Key Words 1   **Circle.**

home      family 

dining room       living room 

bedroom       kitchen 

Ready to Read: Nonfiction

1 Key Words 2 **Match.**

water

garden

stove

bed

2 Trace. Circle.

g a r d e n

r o o m

s t o v e

b e d

3 Match. Color.

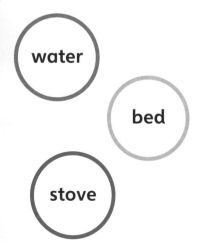

water

bed

stove

Reading Strategy: Comparing

1 **What's different? Circle.**

2 **Read** with your teacher's help. **What's similar? What's different?**

Big and Small

I'm Anna.

Look at my dollhouse!
It's big. It has a kitchen,
living room, and a bedroom.
Look at the bed. It's small!

I'm Philly.

Look at my tree house!
It's one room. It isn't big.
It has a small table and four
chairs. My friends and I
play here!

3 Match.

4 Circle.

It's small.

It's big.

It isn't small.

It isn't big.

5 Imagine. Draw your treehouse.

Prepositions: *in, on, under*

Where's the stove?	It's **in** the kitchen.
Where's the doll?	It's **on** the chair.
Where are the toys?	They're **under** the bed.

1 Match.

in

on

under

2 Circle *in, on,* or *under.*

He is **on** / **under**
the table.

She is **on** / **under**
the bed.

They are **on** / **in**
the kitchen.

3 Draw. Color.

 on

 under

 in

66

4 Match.

The robot is on the table.   The cars are under the bed.

The dinosaurs are in the box.   The ball is under the chair.

5 Trace.

It's on the chair.   It's in the garden.   It's under the box.

My Life

What's in your bedroom? Draw and color.

1 **Say. Color.**

nut   wig

 cut

 big

dig

hut

2 **Say. Circle.**

a (nut)   (hut)   wig   b big   dig   but
c wig   cut   Stig   d big   but   nut

3 **Say. Color.**

cut	wig
hut	Stig

nut	big
dig	but

wig	big
nut	hut

1 **Trace. Match.**

Let's play.

It's my turn.

It's your turn.

Nouns

A noun is a place, a person, an animal, or an object.

1 **Match.**

fish

apartment

chair

boy

place
person
animal
object

2 **Circle.**

place

gym

pencils

person

cat

girl

animal

hut

turtle

object

teacher

toy

3 **Cross out X.**

place	b~~oy~~	school	garden
person	girl	home	family
animal	cat	water	turtle
object	bed	chair	teacher

① **Mark ✓ the nouns. Trace.**

These are nouns.

box ☑   small ☐

green ☐   stairs ☐

stove ☐   blue ☐

big ☐   book ☐

roof ☐   yellow ☐

② **Trace the nouns. Match.**

big garden

big tree

small house

red roof

blue stairs

1 Key Words 4 **Match.**

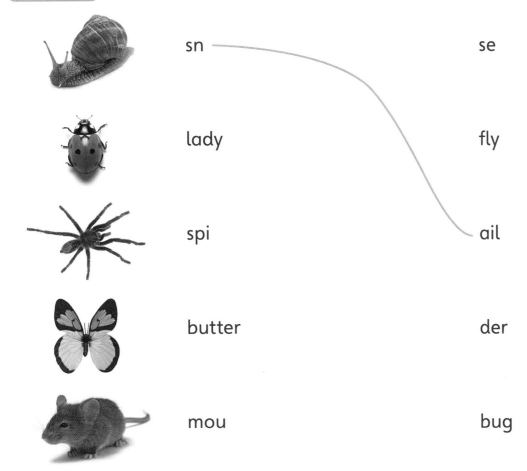

sn   se

lady   fly

spi   ail

butter   der

mou   bug

2 **Color.**

butterfly   forest   ladybug

1 Circle the setting. Color.

2 Read with your teacher's help.

Mouse Helps Butterfly

SB pages 83–88

③ Match in order.

④ Circle the story setting.

Verb *to be*: *Yes/No* Questions

Is **the snail in the water?**   Yes, it is.
Is **the spider under the bed?**   No, it isn't.

1 **Circle.**

Is the butterfly in the garden?

(Yes, it is.)   No, it isn't.

Is the turtle in the water?

Yes, it is.   No, it isn't.

Is the snail on the rock?

Yes, it is.   No, it isn't.

Is the cat in the tree?

Yes, it is.   No, it isn't.

2 **Match.**

Is the ladybug under the box?

Yes, it is.

No, it isn't.

Is the ladybug on the apple?

Yes, it is.

No, it isn't.

Is the cat in the box?

Yes, it is.

No, it isn't.

Is the cat on the chair?

Yes, it is.

No, it isn't.

3 **Circle.**

Is the butterfly big?   Yes, it is. / No, it isn't.

Is the spider black?   Yes, it is. / No, it isn't.

Is the mouse happy?   Yes, it is. / No, it isn't.

4 Circle.

Is he on the stairs?　　Yes, he is. / No, he isn't.

Is she in her bedroom?　　Yes, she is. / No, she isn't.

Are they in the kitchen?　　Yes, they are. / No, they aren't.

5 Trace.

Is the mouse on the house?　　Yes, it is. No, it isn't.

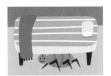

Is the spider under the bed?　　Yes, it is. No, it isn't.

Is the butterfly in a box?　　Yes, it is. No, it isn't.

My Life

Draw your home. Mark ✓.

Is it a tree house?　☐ Yes, it is.
　　　　　　　　　☐ No, it isn't.

Is it an apartment?　☐ Yes, it is.
　　　　　　　　　☐ No, it isn't.

Is it a house?　☐ Yes, it is.
　　　　　☐ No, it isn't.

1 Who's helping others? Circle.

2 Match.

Mairi helps in the garden.

Omar helps in the kitchen.

Asya helps in her bedroom.

Jack helps in the living room.

3 Draw yourself helping at home.

I help my family.

The Big Challenge and Oracy

How can I describe my home?

Answer with your teacher's help.

Color or  .

1 I made a big envelope.   **or**

2 I drew my home.   **or**

3 I described my home.   **or**

Oracy

Check Your Oracy!

1 I took turns.	**Yes / No**
2 I said "It's your turn."	**Yes / No**

Home is my mom, dad, and sister.

1 **Match.**

bedroom   bathroom   garden

dining room   living room   kitchen

2 **Write.**

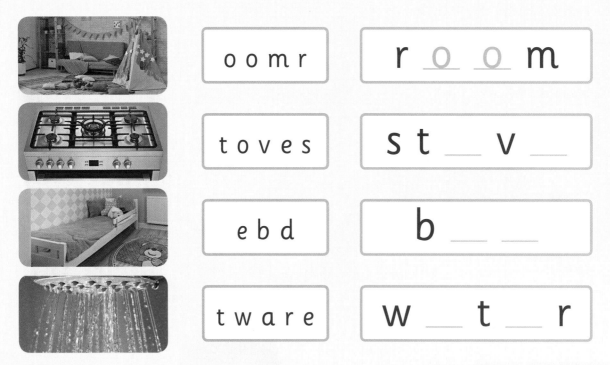

o o m r	r <u>o</u> o m
t o v e s	s t _ v _
e b d	b _ _ _
t w a r e	w _ t _ r

3 **Match. Trace.**

r o o f

s t a i r s

4 **Draw a ball. Color.**

 in

 on

 under

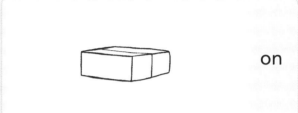 on

5 **Circle.**

Is the fish in the water?

~~Yes, it is.~~

No, it isn't.

Is the snail under the chair?

Yes, it is.

No, it isn't.

Is the ladybug under the leaf?

Yes, it is.

No, it isn't.

Is the cat in the box?

Yes, it is.

No, it isn't.

6 **Match.**

boy

toy

mouse

apartment

animal place person object

1 **Cross out X.**

socks

T-shirt

hat

jacket

skirt

glasses

2 **Match.**

What color is the T-shirt?   It's green.

Is the T-shirt on the chair?   No, it isn't.

What color is the hat?   It's purple.

Is the hat on the chair?   Yes, it is.

3 **Number 1, 2, and 3.**

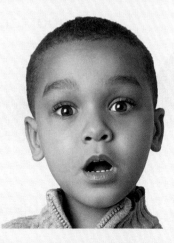

1 I can't find my glasses!

_____ Are your glasses on the table?

_____ Yes, they are.

What can you remember about ... Unit 4?

1 **Circle.**

They're in the
living room / kitchen.

2 **Match.**

          butter   bug

          lady   fly

3 **Match the similar sounds.**

cut   big   dig
wig   but   hut

4 **Circle the nouns.**

teacher   happy   tall
kitchen   boy   rabbit

5 **Mark ✓.**

It's under
the chair. ☐

It's on
the chair. ☐

6 **Trace the correct answer.**

Is the house in a tree?

Yes, it is.
No, it isn't.

Check your answers in the Student's Book. How did you do?
5–6 ☐ **Great!** 3–4 ☐ **Good!** 0–2 ☐ **Try harder!**

 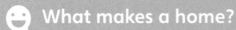 **What makes a home?**

Circle.

5 Where do wild animals belong?

1 ▶ 5.1 **Watch the video.**
Draw the animals to complete the graphic organizer.

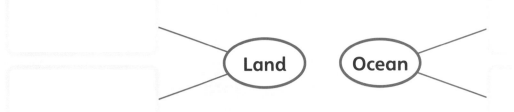

Land   Ocean

2 Key Words 1 **Match.**

zebra

elephant

octopus

dolphin

land

ocean

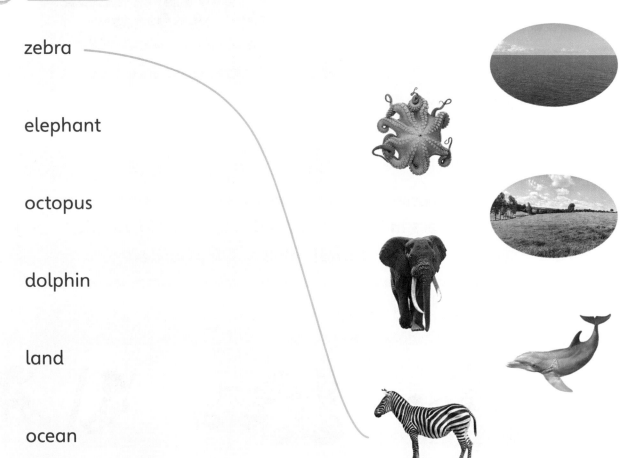

1 Key Words 2 **Color.**

claw

beak

teeth

tail

fur

2 **Trace. Match.**

t e e t h

b e a k

t a i l

c l a w

3 **What can you see in the jungle? Color.**

I see a zebra
in the jungle.

83

Reading Strategy: Visualizing

(1) **What animals is the boy imagining? Draw.**

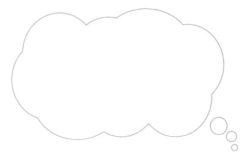

It has big ears.

It has big teeth.

It's black and white.

(2) Read with your teacher's help.

Wild Animals

Pandas are big bears. They have fur. They live in the forest.

A crocodile is a big animal. It has big teeth. It lives in the jungle.

This parrot has red feathers. It has a big beak.

A zebra is black and white. It has a long tail.

③ Match

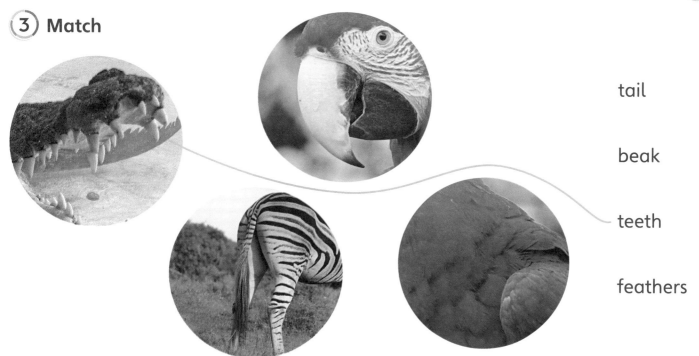

tail

beak

teeth

feathers

④ Circle.

(Ocean)   (Land)

whale   elephant   bear   octopus

⑤ Match. Color.

small teeth

big claws

small eyes

short tail

brown fur

Verb *to be*: *Wh-* Questions

What are **they**?

What **color** are **the dolphins**?

Where are **they**?

They are **dolphins**.

They're **gray**.

They're **in the ocean**.

1 Match.

What are they?

What color are they?

Where are they?

They're in the tree.

They're brown.

They're bears.

What is it?

What color is it?

Where is it?

It's in the ocean.

It's a fish.

It's blue and green.

2 Circle.

Where is it?	What are they?	What color is it?

It's in the forest.	They're zebras.	It's black and white.
It's in the house.	They're elephants.	It's brown and white.

3 Trace.

What's your name?

Where are you?

86

4 Match.

| What's your name? |
| How old are you? |
| What color is it? |
| What are they? |

It's green.

Usi.

I'm **6**.

They're spiders.

5 Color.

Where / What — is it? — It's a turtle.

How / Where — old is it? — It's 100 years old.

Where / What — is it? — It's in the ocean.

My Life

Trace. Answer.

What's your favorite wild animal? _____

Where does it live? _____

1 Say. Color.

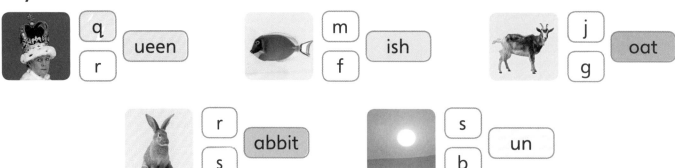

q / r ueen

m / f ish

j / g oat

r / s abbit

s / b un

2 Which one is different? Cross out X.

a song   sun   ~~tin~~   d ring   rabbit   fish

b queen   jaws   quiz   e jaws   song   jar

c jar   goat   gate

3 Say. Match.

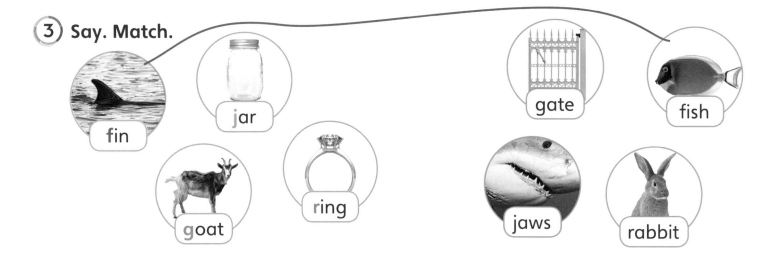

fin   jar   ring   goat

gate   fish   jaws   rabbit

1 Who is participating actively? Circle.

Let's play!

No!

Let's run!

OK!

Identifying Questions and Exclamations

Question: What color is the fish?
Exclamation: That's good!

1 Circle. (?) (!)

Look (!)
What is it(?)
Is it a mouse?
No, it's a rabbit!
Where's the rabbit?

Look!
Are they dolphins?
Yes!
Where are they?
They're in the ocean.
Dolphins are my favorite animal!

2 Color.

Question ?   Exclamation !

Look!

Is it a bird?

Yes!

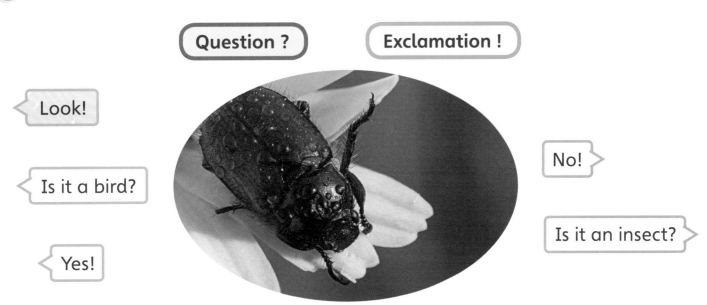

No!

Is it an insect?

1 **Trace.**

What is it ?

It's a snake !

Don't touch !

Is it in the ocean ?

No, it isn't !

Is it in the tree ?

Yes, it is !

2 **Color.**

[?] [!]

Look [?] [!]

Are they tigers [?] [!]   They are cheetahs [?] [!]

No, they aren't [?] [!]   Are they fast [?] [!]

What are they [?] [!]   Yes, they are [?] [!]

1 Key Words 4 **Look. Match.**

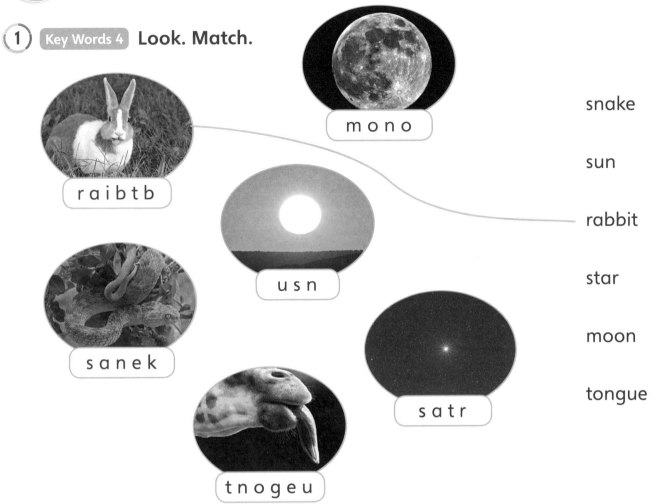

m o n o

r a i b t b

u s n

s a n e k

t n o g e u

s a t r

snake

sun

rabbit

star

moon

tongue

2 **Color.**

star

snake

tongue

moon

Reading Strategy: Predicting from Pictures

1 **What comes next? Circle.**

a  |  |

b  |  |

2 **Read** with your teacher's help.

They're in the Water!

Rabbit and Snake are in a boat.

They are looking at the moon.
They see a star.

The moon jumps into the water!

The star jumps into the water!

Rabbit and Snake are surprised.

The star and the moon are playing
in the water.

Snake says, "Jump off my tongue!"

Rabbit says, "They're having fun!"

3 Circle *Yes* or *No*.

a The star is in the .   Yes   (No)

b The moon jumps into the  .   Yes   No

c Rabbit and Snake are in the .   Yes   No

4 Who says it? Circle.

Jump off my tongue!

They're having fun!

5 What comes next? Color.

Verb *to be*: Yes/No Questions

Are the animals in the forest?   Yes, they are.
Are they in the water?   No, they aren't.

1 **Match.**

   Are the dolphins in the water?   Yes, they are.

   Are the lions in the jungle?   No, they aren't.

   Are the giraffes in the tree?   Yes, they are.

2 **Circle.**

Are the zebras in the ocean?
   Yes, they are.
No, they aren't.

Are the pandas in the forest?
   Yes, they are.
No, they aren't.

Are the parrots in the tree?
   Yes, they are.
No, they aren't.

Are the rabbits in the water?
   Yes, they are.
No, they aren't.

3 **Draw.**

Are the blue whales in the water?

Yes, they are.

(4) Color.

Are they brown?
Yes, they are.

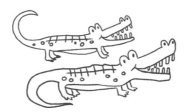
Are they yellow?
No, they aren't.

Are they orange?
Yes, they are.

(5) Trace.

Are they black and white?

Yes, they are.
No, they aren't.

Are they red?

Yes, they are.
No, they aren't.

Are they in the jungle?

Yes, they are.
No, they aren't.

My Life

What's your favorite ocean animal? Draw.

1 Is this good for animals? Mark ✓.

a  ✓

b  ☐

c  ☐

d  ☐

2 Match.

Let's take care of animals' homes!

3 How do you take care of animals? Draw.

The Big Challenge and Oracy

How can we describe a wild animal?

Answer with your teacher's help.

Color 🙂 **or** 🙁 .

1 I made an animal mask. **or**

2 I described the animal. **or**

3 I told the class about my animal. 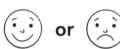 **or**

Oracy

Check Your Oracy!

1 I participated.	Yes / No	
2 I used the cue card.	Yes / No	
3 I listened to my partner.	Yes / No	

Let's be butterflies!

1 **Circle. Match.**

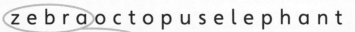

z e b r a o c t o p u s e l e p h a n t

d o l p h i n r a b b i t s n a k e

2 **Mark ✓.**

teeth ✓   tail ☐

claws ☐   tongue ☐

feathers ☐   beak ☐

tongue ☐   fur ☐

3 **Trace.**

f e a t h e r s

i n s e c t s

4 Color.

What

Where

is it?

It's a snake.

How

Where

is it?

It's in the ocean.

What

Where

color are they?

They're orange.

5 Trace.

Are they snakes?

Yes, they are.

No, they aren't.

Are the rabbits in the water?

Yes, they are.

No, they aren't.

Are they blue?

Yes, they are.

No, they aren't.

Are the dolphins in the ocean?

Yes, they are.

No, they aren't.

6 Color.

Look!

Is it a zebra?

Is it an elephant?

What is it?

No, it's not!

Yes!

SPEAKING MISSION

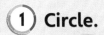

1 Circle.

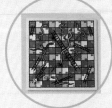    

board game   dice   win

square   game piece   lose

2 Match.

   Are you a tiger?   Yes, I am.

   Are you a rabbit?   Yes, I am.

   Are you a zebra?   No, I'm not.

3 Number 1, 2, 3, and 4.

__1__ What's this?

_____ It's a board game.

_____ Throw the dice!

_____ I win!

What can you remember about ... Unit 5?

1 Match.

It's

a dolphin.

an elephant.

an octopus.

2 Mark ✓.

It's ☐ in the ocean.
☐ on land.

3 Circle the questions.

What are they?   Look!

Let's play!   Is it a bird?

4 Match.

song   ring
fins   sun
rabbit   fish

5 Circle.

Ketzi paints with
her **tail / tongue**.

6 Circle.

moon   sun

Check your answers in the Student's Book. How did you do?
5–6 ☐ Great!   3–4 ☐ Good!   0–2 ☐ Try harder!

? 😊 Where do wild animals belong?

Draw.

6   What can people do?

1 ▶ 6.1 **Watch the video. Draw to complete the graphic organizer.**

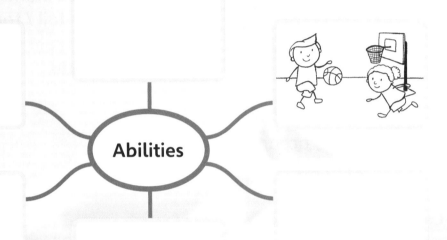

Abilities

2 Key Words 1 **Trace. Match.**

a b i l i t y

p a i n t

r u n

s k a t e

t a l k

p l a y   b a s k e t b a l l

1 Key Words 2 **Circle.**

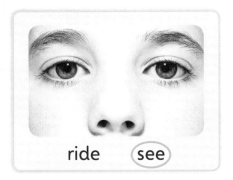

ride   (see)

c – a – t
cat

swim   spell

climb   see

spell   ride

My name is Amira.

say   climb

ride   swim

2 **Trace. Match.**

BOY

boy, b-o-y, boy

I'm six years old

ride

climb

see

say

swim

spell

Reading Strategy: Predicting from Titles

1 **Match.**

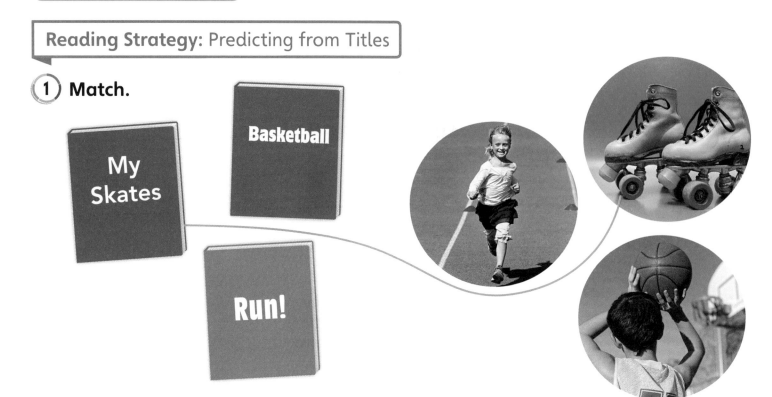

2 **Read** with your teacher's help.

Kids with Amazing Abilities

This is Sam. He is 6. He is from Canada. Sam can swim very fast. He wins the swimming race!

This is Zehra. She is 7.
She is from Turkey.
She can climb. Look at Zehra!
She's climbing the rock.

Francie is blind. She can't see. But she can read! She is reading a book for blind people.

What can you do? What is your amazing ability?

3 Circle.

I can swim.   (I can't swim.)

I can climb.   I can't climb.

I can see.   I can't see.

I can read.   I can't read.

4 Color.

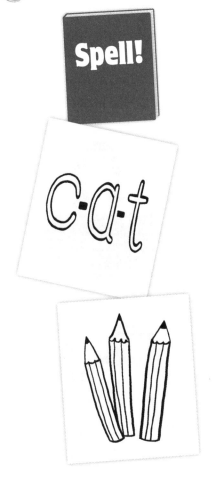

Spell!

c·a·t

I Can Paint!

Let's Swim!

I can ... / I can't ...

 I can skate.    I can't skate.

① **Mark ✓ or ✗.**

can ✓   can't ✗

② **Match.**

I can draw.

I can spell.

I can play.

I can't run.

③ **Trace.**

I **can** run.   I **can't** paint.

4 Circle.

I **can** / **can't** write words backwards.

I **can** / **can't** climb.

I **can** / **can't** skate.

I **can** / **can't** swim.

5 Write *can* or *can't*.

I ___can___ skate. ✓

I _____ climb. ✓

I _____ run. ✗

My Life

What can you do? Circle.

(1) Say. Trace.

h t p m b d

h o p

d a d

p o p

m a d

b a d

t o p

(2) Say. Cross out ✗ the different sound.

a hat   hop   b~~ad~~
b bad   top   box
c mad   dad   doll

d pet   pop   hop
e toy   mad   top
f hat   box   hop

(1) Circle.

Do you agree?

Swimming is difficult.

Yes!   No!

Running is easy.

Yes!   No!

Spelling is fun!

h – o – p
hop

HOP

Yes!   No!

Verbs

A verb can tell about an action.

ride

eat

1 **Circle the verbs. Match.**

s w i m t e e t h p a i n t j u m p s c h o o l b a g s k a t e

2 **Cross out X.**

not a verb X

happy

jump

tired

play

book

read

3 **Trace the verbs.**

pencil eat see blue swim ladybug

4 Match.

a noun ———————— draw

verb ———————— pencil

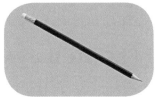

b noun ———————— play

verb ———————— teacher

5 Write.

(s a k t e) Can you _____skate_____ ?

(n r u) I can't _____ !

(j m u p) Can you _____ ?

(c m l i b) I can _____ !

1 **Circle.**

puppy

dancer

read

music

love

practice

2 Key Words 4   **Write. Match.**

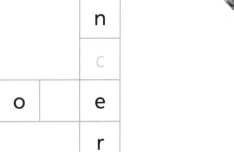

		d		
r		a	d	

n

c

l	o		e	

r

p

m	u		i	c

p	r	a	c		i	c	e

y

Reading Strategy: Cause and Effect

1 **Draw the effect.**

Cause   Effect

2 **Read** with your teacher's help.

Practice!

Ina and Azra are sisters.
Ina can't dance. She's sad.

Azra can't play music. She's sad.

Ina practices every day.
Azra practices every day.

Azra can play music. Ina is a dancer.
Everyone claps! They're happy!

Explore the Text

(3) Number 1, 2, and 3.

a

b

(4) Match.

a Ina can't dance.

b Azra can't play music.

c Azra practices.

d Ina practices.

(5) Circle the effect.

a

b

Yes/No Questions with *can* and *can't*

Can **he** see?
No, he can't.

Can **it** climb?
Yes, it can.

(1) **Circle.**

Can she swim?
Yes, she can. / No, she can't.

Can he play basketball?
Yes, he can. / No, he can't.

Can she drive?
Yes, she can. / No, she can't.

Can he walk?
Yes, he can. / No, he can't.

(2) **Match.**

Can it
dance?

Can she
roller-skate?

Can he
ride?

Can it
climb?

Yes, it can.

Yes, she can.

No, it can't.

Yes, he can.

(3) **Trace.**

Can it talk? No, it can't.

114

4 **Circle.**

	📖	🎨
Yamir	✓	✗
Elsa	✗	✓

Can Yamir read?
Yes, he can. / No, he can't.

Can Elsa read?
Yes, she can. / No, she can't.

Can Elsa paint?
Yes, she can. / No, she can't.

Can Yamir paint?
Yes, he can. / No, he can't.

5 **Trace.**

Can you climb?

Yes, I can.
No, I can't.

Can they ride?

Yes, they can.
No, they can't.

Can he swim?

Yes, he can.
No, he can't.

My Life

What is your amazing ability? Draw.

I can ...

1 Match.

Why do they practice?

To paint well.

To skate well.

To dance well.

To play basketball well.

To read well.

2 How can they do better? Trace.

They p r a c t i c e.

3 What do you practice? Draw.

Practice is good!

The Big Challenge

What different things can we do?

Answer with your teacher's help.

Color  **or** 😞 .

1 I made my spinner. **or**

2 I said 3 things I can do. **or**

3 I said 3 things I can't do. **or**

Can you ride?

Oracy

Check Your Oracy!

1 I listened to others.	**Yes / No**	
2 I agreed or disagreed.	**Yes / No**	
3 I respected my classmates' opinions.	**Yes / No**	

Do you agree?

1 Match.

climb

ride

run

paint

swim

2 Circle.

music   love

cat   puppy

dancer   blind

ride   read

3 Trace.

Can you walk
b a c k w a r d s ?

4 Circle.

Dora is blind.
She **can** / **can't** see.

She **can** / **can't**
read with her
hands.

She **can** / **can't**
ride a bike.

She **can** / **can't**
play.

5 Trace. Match.

Lola can   skate.

Lola can't   ride.

Gib can   climb.

Gib can't   dance.

6 Color.

verbs

spell   puppy   talk   orange

        ability   zebra

    read   write

1 **Match.**

tag

marbles

board games

telephone

hopscotch

hide-and-seek

2 **Do you agree? Circle.**

Board games are fun.	Yes!	No!
Hopscotch is boring.	Yes!	No!
Tag is boring!	Yes!	No!
Hide-and-seek is fun!	Yes!	No!

3 **Number 1, 2, 3 and 4.**

_1_ Let's play tag!

_4_ Yes! Hopscotch is fun!

____ Let's play hopscotch!

____ No! Tag is boring!

120

What can you remember about ... Unit 6?

1 **Circle.**

Yan **can / can't** read.

2 **Match.**

skate

play
basketball

climb

3 **Circle.**

He **can / can't** see.

4 **Mark ✓.**

Can you ride?

Yes, I can.

No, I can't.

5 **Circle the verbs.**

run   happy   swim
girl   spell   talk

6 **Trace.**

h o p   b a d

m a d   t o p

d a d   p o p

7 **Circle.**

Hanna is a **ballet /
hip-hop** dancer.

8 **Circle.**

marbles   hopscotch

Check your answers in the Student's Book. How did you do?

6–8 ☐ Great!   3–5 ☐ Good!   0–2 ☐ Try harder!

? 😃 **What can you do?**

Circle.

Is all food healthy?

1 ▶ 7.1 **Watch the video. Draw to complete the graphic organizer.**

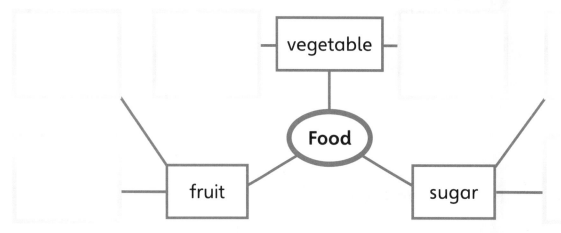

vegetable

Food

fruit

sugar

2 Key Words 1 **Trace. Circle.**

b a n a n a   v e g e t a b l e

s u g a r   f r u i t

g r a p e   s p i n a c h

1 Key Words 2 **Circle. Match.**

e	w	a	t	e	r	b
m	k	l	p	o	i	l
r	i	s	b	a	c	a
w	j	u	i	c	e	p
y	o	g	u	r	t	g
r	a	p	u	b	a	n
t	o	m	a	t	o	j

2 **Trace.**

t o m a t o   o i l   w a t e r

y o g u r t   j u i c e   r i c e

3 **Draw. Color.**

juice    tomato   yogurt

Reading Strategy: Similarities and Differences

1 **Fruit or vegetable? Circle.**

Different   Same

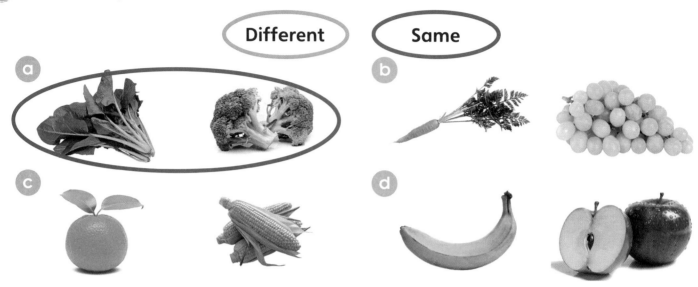

2 **Read** with your teacher's help.

My Favorite Snack

I'm Anita. I love popsicles! I make them with yogurt and bananas. Popsicles are delicious!

I'm Brian. I don't like meat. But I love vegetables! I make sandwiches with tomatoes. Tomato sandwiches are my favorite snack!

I'm Lisa. My mom makes fried rice. She cooks it in oil. I love fried rice! It has vegetables and meat. It's delicious!

3 Match.

I love popsicles!

I don't like meat.

I love fried rice!

4 Match.

I love vegetables
with fried rice!

Tomato sandwiches
are my favorite snack!

Popsicles are delicious!

Grammar in Context

Like / don't like

I like spinach.

I don't like vegetables.

(1) What do they like? Write ✓ or X.

 ✓

(2) What does he like? Circle.

I like vegetables. I don't like fruit.

(3) Trace.

I like vegetables.   I don't like sugar.

126

4 Color.

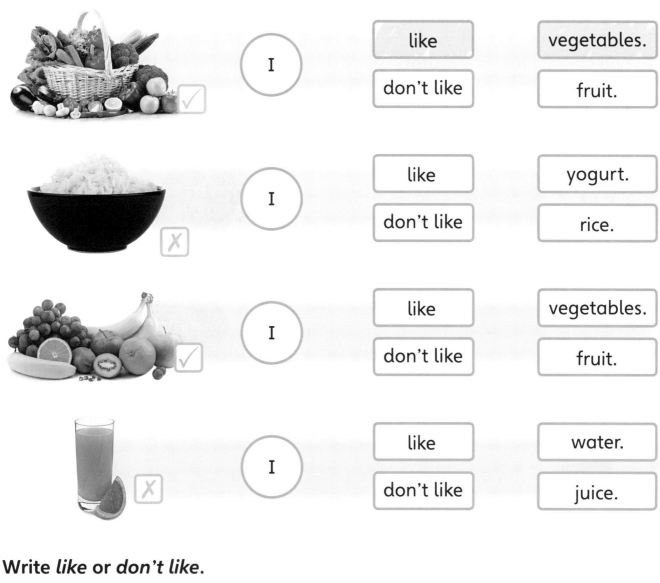

I | like | vegetables.
| don't like | fruit.

I | like | yogurt.
| don't like | rice.

I | like | vegetables.
| don't like | fruit.

I | like | water.
| don't like | juice.

5 Write *like* or *don't like*.

I _____ fruit. ✓

I _____ yogurt. ✗

My Life

What do you like? Circle.

(1) Say. Color.

(b) (m) (x)

box	fox	arm
arm	jam	tub

tub	fox	cub
Bob	jam	arm

(2) Trace. Match.

a **cub**

b **box**

c **jam**

d **fox**

(3) Write b, m, or x.

 f o _x_

 t u ____

 j a ____

 c u ____

(1) Trace.

Good job!

Thank you!

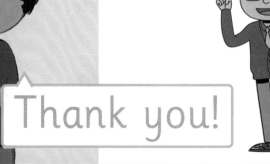

Adjectives

Adjectives describe people, places, or things.

happy   young

(1) Match.

short
red
old
slow
green

(2) Cross out X.

toy   yellow

X
not an adjective

happy   girl

apples   four

hair   short

delicious   eat

(3) Trace the adjectives.

two   vegetables   old

tall   happy   fruit

4 Color.

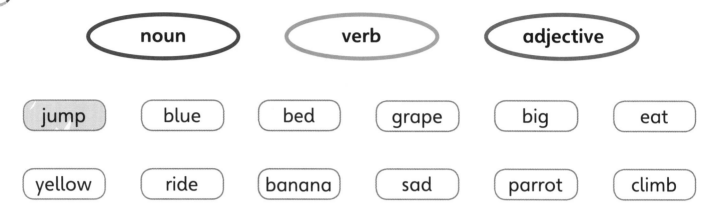

noun   verb   adjective

jump   blue   bed   grape   big   eat

yellow   ride   banana   sad   parrot   climb

5 Draw. Color.

| an orange vegetable | three green grapes |

| a happy boy | two blue butterflies |

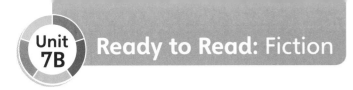

1 Key Words 4 **Circle.**

(broccoli) sugar 　　　 soup fish 　　　 rice French fries

chocolate spinach 　　 juice soup 　　 muffin yogurt

2 **Match. Trace.**

bliccoro 　　　　　　 muffin

suop 　　　　　　 chocolate

cohocalte 　　　　　　 fish

fhis 　　　　　　 French fries

Fenrhc riesf 　　　　　　 soup

mufifn 　　　　　　 broccoli

Reading Strategy: Main Idea

(1) **What is the main idea? Circle.**

Kim's healthy lunch

Kim's favorite color

Kim's unhealthy lunch

(2) **Read** with your teacher's help.

Lunchtime

Mark is at Matt's home.
Mark says, "I'm hungry."
Matt says, "Let's make lunch."

"Do you like soup?"
"No, I don't," says Mark.
"Do you like fish?"
"No, I don't."
"Do you like broccoli?"
"No, I don't."

"Do you like French fries?"
"No, I don't."
Matt says, "OK. What do you like?"
"I like sandwiches. I like chocolate."

"Let's make chocolate sandwiches!"
"Yes!"

③ Number 1, 2, 3, and 4.

1

④ What's the main idea? Color.

Matt's home

Matt and Mark's breakfast

Mark's favorite snack

⑤ Match.

French fries

broccoli

sandwiches

fish

soup

chocolate

Yes/No Questions with *like*

Do you like muffins?
Yes, I do. / No, I don't.

1 Match.

like you broccoli ? Do

you like Do soup ?

muffins ? you like Do

Do ? fruit like you

Do you like muffins?

Do you like broccoli?

Do you like fruit?

Do you like soup?

2 Circle.

Do you like ? ✓   (Yes, I do.)   No, I don't.

Do you like ? ✗   Yes, I do.   No, I don't.

Do you like ? ✓   Yes, I do.   No, I don't.

Do you like ? ✗   Yes, I do.   No, I don't.

3 What do you like? Color.

Do you like soup?	Do you like rice?	Do you like fish?
Yes, I do. No, I don't.	Yes, I do. No, I don't.	Yes, I do. No, I don't.

4 Trace.

Do you like broccoli?

Yes, I do.
No, I don't.

Do you like spinach?

Yes, I do.
No, I don't.

5 Circle.

Do you like grapes?

Yes, I do.

No, I don't.

Do you like rice?

Yes, I do.

No, I don't.

My Life

Draw 2 foods you like.

Draw 2 foods you don't like.

1 What is healthy food? Mark ✓.

2 Circle.

healthy   unhealthy

3 What healthy food do you eat? Draw.

I like healthy food.

The Big Challenge and Oracy

How can we make a healthy dessert?

Answer with your teacher's help.

Color or 😕 .

1 I found an easy recipe. **or**

2 I wrote and drew it. **or**

3 I described it to the class. **or**

My healthy dessert!

Oracy

Check Your Oracy!

1 I spoke clearly.	Yes / No
2 I said *Good job!* to my classmates.	Yes / No
3 I said *Thank you* to my classmates.	Yes / No

Good job!

1 Match.

banana

broccoli

spinach

grapes

apple

tomato

2 Trace. Match.

juice

fish

vegetables

yogurt

French fries

soup

3 Circle.

vegetables   fruit

sugar   rice

French fries   muffin

138

4 **Circle.**

I **like** / **don't** like chocolate.

I **like** / **don't** like soup.

I **like** / **don't** like French fries.

I **like** / **don't** like rice.

5 **Trace.**

Do you like grapes?

Yes, I do.
No, I don't.

Do you like muffins?

Yes, I do.
No, I don't.

Do you like yogurt?

Yes, I do.
No, I don't.

Do you like broccoli?

Yes, I do.
No, I don't.

6 **Color.**

two   oil   happy   small   adjectives   rice   tomato   fruit   green

SPEAKING MISSION

(1) Match.

lollipop

cookie

potato chips

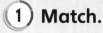

corn

bread

tomato

(2) Circle.

How much is the corn?	How much is the lollipop?	Can I have a cookie, please?
I dollar	2 dollars	
(It's one dollar.)	It's one dollar.	Thank you!
It's two dollars.	It's two dollars.	Here you go!

(3) Number 1, 2, 3, and 4.

_1_ Can I have a lollipop, please?

____ Here you go!

____ How much is it?

____ It's one dollar.

140

What can you remember about ... Unit 7?

① **Circle.**

 I like / don't like ✓ water.

② **Circle.**

 I like / don't like ✗ bananas.

③ **Match.**

broccoli

grapes

spinach

④ **Circle the adjectives.**

juice   long   delicious

fruit   small   eat

⑤ **Match x, m, and b.**

box   arm

jam   tub

cub   fox

⑥ **Trace.**

 Do you like fruit?

⑦ **Circle.**

cookies   muffins

⑧ **Color the tomato.**

Check your answers in the Student's Book. How did you do?

6–8 ☐ **Great!**   3–5 ☐ **Good!**   0–2 ☐ **Try harder!**

? 😊 **Is all food healthy?**

Circle.

Yes.   No.

8 Are routines important?

1 ▶ 8.1 **Watch the video. Draw to complete the graphic organizer.**

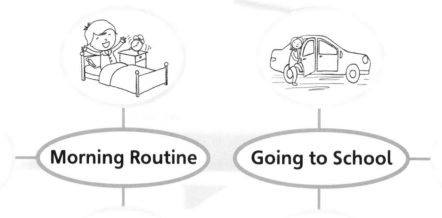

( ) — **Morning Routine**   **Going to School** — ( )

( )   ( )

2 Key Words 1 **Trace. Match.**

g o   to school

e a t   breakfast

b r u s h   my teeth

w a l k

r i d e   my bike

t a k e   the bus

Unit 8A Ready to Read: Nonfiction
8A

1 Key Words 2 **Color.**

 a — take · my hands · a bath

 b — change · my clothes · exercise

 c — wash · fun · my hands

 d — do · my clothes · exercise

 e — have · fun · the bus

2 Trace. Number.

1 I change my clothes.
2 I eat breakfast.
3 I brush my teeth.
4 I go to school.

 8:00
 7:15
 7:30
 7:45

143

SB pages 162–63

Reading Strategy: Summarizing

1 **Mark the best summary** ✓.

My name is Susan.

At 7:15, I change my clothes.

At 7:30, I eat breakfast.

At 7:45, I brush my teeth.

I go to school at 8:00.

The text is about …

Susan's breakfast. ☐   Susan's morning routine. ☐

2 **Read with your teacher's help.**

ALL BLOGS   MY BLOG   NEW POST   SEARCH:

My Routine After School

My name is Cara.

This is my routine after school.

I'm hungry after school. I eat a healthy snack.

I change my clothes. I wear my favorite shoes.

Then, I play with my brother, Paul. We have fun.

After we play, we eat dinner. Before dinner, we wash our hands.

After dinner, I take a bath.

Then, I go to bed. Good night!

Me!
snack
my brother
my favorite shoes
broccoli again
Bubbles!

144

(3) Number in order.

1 I eat a healthy snack.

2 I wear my favorite shoes.

3 I play with my brother.

4 We wash our hands.

5 We eat dinner.

6 I take a bath.

7 I go to bed.

1

(4) Mark ✓ the best summary.

This text is about …

Cara's morning routine. ☐

Cara's after-school routine. ☐

Cara's healthy snack. ☐

(5) Trace. Match.

 we play, we eat dinner.

Before dinner, we wash our hands.

Grammar in Context

Present Simple: Affirmative

I walk **to school.**

(1) Match.

| I ride my bike. | I take the bus. | I wash my hands. | I do exercise. | I sleep ten hours. |

(2) What do they do after school? Circle.

I wash my hands.

I brush my teeth.

I sleep.

I do exercise.

I have fun.

I go to school.

I ride my bike.

I walk home.

I take the bus.

I ride my bike.

(3) Trace.

I sleep ten hours.   I brush my teeth.

146

4 Color.

I walk to school.

I change my clothes.

I do exercise.

I take the bus.

5 Color.

a

I | take | to school.
walk

b

I | take | the bus.
wash

c

I | ride | my teeth.
brush

d

I | do | exercise.
eat

> **My Life**

What do you do after school? Circle.

1 Say. Color.

(st)   (**sk**)   (nt)

| nest | ant | fast | desk | cent | mask |

2 Write *sk*, *st*, or *nt*.

a <u>n</u> <u>t</u>   n e __ __   c e __ __   m a __ __

3 Trace. Draw.

fast

desk

cent

nest

ant

mask

1 What does the boy ask? Circle.

Thank you.

Can you repeat that?

Statements

A statement tells us something.   **I have fun in school.**

1 **Circle.**

Find the statements.

I eat breakfast.

Can you ride a bike?

walk

I do exercise.

I brush my teeth.

my school

2 **Cross out X.**

I brush my teeth.
my teeth

X
not a statement

school
I like school.

good exercise
Exercise is good.

I like breakfast.
I like

after school
I play after school.

3 **Trace the statements.**

I take a bath.   We have breakfast.

4 **Trace. Draw.**

After school,

I change my clothes.

I play.

I brush my teeth.

I go to bed.

5 **Match. Trace.**

I eat   to school.

I ride   my bike.

I have   breakfast.

I go   fun.

Ready to Read: Fiction

1 | Key Words 4 | **Trace.**

 carry

 wake up

 march

 clean

 collect

 find

2 **What do you collect? Draw.**

dolls   coins   toys   shells

I collect ...

Reading Strategy: Making Judgments

1 **Match.**

It's good.

It's bad.

2 **Read** with your teacher's help.

Rabbit Food?

1

Wake up! Let's find food!

Mama Rabbit wakes up Robbie. They are hungry.

2

Carrots are delicious!

I don't like vegetables.

Mama Rabbit and Robbie go to the garden. They find some spinach and carrots. But Robbie isn't happy.

3

Let's collect fruit.

I love fruit!

Mom says "OK. Let's collect fruit."

Robbie sees some grapes. He loves grapes! They collect a lot of grapes.

4

Can you carry that?

Yes, I can!

5

Let's eat breakfast!

Yes, I'm hungry!

Explore the Text

(3) **Match.**

Let's find   carry that?

I don't   food.

I love   like vegetables!

Can you   I can.

Yes,   fruit.

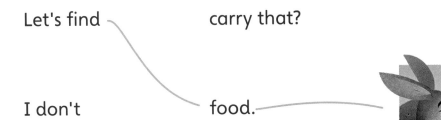

(4) **Match.**

Carrots are delicious!

I don't like vegetables.

Yes, I'm hungry!

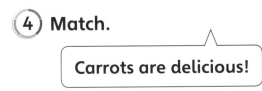

Let's eat breakfast!

I love fruit!

(5) **What's Robbie's favorite food? Trace.**

He loves fruit!

Present Simple: Negative

I **don't walk** to school.

I **don't eat French fries.**

1 Affirmative or negative? Mark ✓ or ✗.

I **don't take the bus.**

 ✗

I **eat breakfast.**

 ☐

☐

I **don't like broccoli.**

I carry my schoolbag. ☐

2 Color.

I | collect | shells.
| don't collect |

I | wake up | at 7.
| don't wake up |

I | brush | my teeth
| don't brush |

I | play | sports.
| don't play |

3 Match.

don't / I / snacks / eat — I don't play in the park.

don't / clean / table / the / I — I don't eat snacks.

I / play / don't / in the park — I don't clean the table.

4 Write.

take   collect   eat

I don't _____
a bath.

I _____
dolls.

I don't _____
cake.

5 Trace what they do or don't do.

I   march
    don't march

with friends.

I   do
    don't do

exercise.

I   make
    don't make

cookies.

My Life

**What do you do
before you go
to bed? Draw.**

1 How can you stay healthy? Mark ✓.

2 What's healthy? Color.

3 What are your healthy habits? Draw.

I do exercise.

How can we describe our routines?

The Big Challenge and Oracy

Answer with your teacher's help.

Color or  .

Monday morning
- get dressed
- brush my teeth
- eat breakfast
- walk to school

1 I talked about things I do. or

2 I made a poster about my routine. or

3 I described my routine. or

Oracy

Check Your Oracy!	
1 I spoke up.	**Yes / No**
2 I used the cue cards.	**Yes / No**

1 Match.

take   my teeth

brush   the bus

eat   a bath

take   to school

go   breakfast

2 Circle.

ride   my bike
        the bus

change   my shoes
           my clothes

wash   my hands
        my bike

have   a bath
        fun

3 Trace.

 find    carry

 wake up    walk

8

(4) Match.

| How do you go to school? |

I / the / bus / take   I ride my bike.

bike / I / my / don't ride   I don't take the bus.

I / don't / the / take / bus   I don't ride my bike.

ride / bike / I / my   I take the bus.

(5) Trace what you do and don't do.

 I brush my teeth.   I don't brush my teeth.

 I eat spinach.   I don't eat spinach.

(6) Color.

a big breakfast   I change my clothes.

I wash my hands.   after school

Statements

I sleep ten hours.   I go to the park.

Do you walk to school?

SPEAKING MISSION

1 **Match.**

1 Take attendance.

2 Raise your hand.

3 Open your books.

4 Be quiet.

5 Put away your book.

6 Take out your pencil.

2 **Circle.**

Stand up, please.

Open your books.

Stand up.

Raise your hand.

3 **Match.**

Let's read.

Hello!

Open your books, please.

Sit down, please.

What can you remember about ... Unit 8?

1 **Color.**

eat

I _____ breakfast.

don't eat

2 **Match.**

 I brush my teeth.

 I wash my hands.

 I have fun.

3 **Mark ✓.**

I play in the park. ☐

I play in my house. ☐

4 **Circle the statement.**

change clothes

I change my clothes.

5 **Match sk, nt, and st.**

desk	cent
ant	mask
fast	nest

6 **Circle.**

Andy Ant **sleeps** / **cleans**.

7 **Trace.**

I collect apples.

8 **Circle.**

wake up

sleep

Check your answers in the Student's Book. How did you do?

6–8 ☐ Great!   3–5 ☐ Good!   0–2 ☐ Try harder!

? **Are routines important?**

Circle.

Yes.   No.

9 Why do we wear different clothes?

1 ▶ 9.1 **Watch the video. Draw to complete the graphic organizer.**

```
        ┌─────────┐                              ┌─────────┐
        │         │                              │         │
        └────┬────┘                              └────┬────┘
             │                                        │
┌─────────┐  │   ╭────────╮   ┌──────────┐   ╭────────╮   ┌─────────┐
│         │──┼──(   Hot    )──│  Clothes  │──(  Cold    )──│         │
└─────────┘  │   ╲ Weather╱   └──────────┘   ╲ Weather╱   └─────────┘
             │                                        │
        ┌────┴────┐                              ┌────┴────┐
        │         │                              │         │
        └─────────┘                              └─────────┘
```

2 **Key Words 1** **Trace. Circle.**

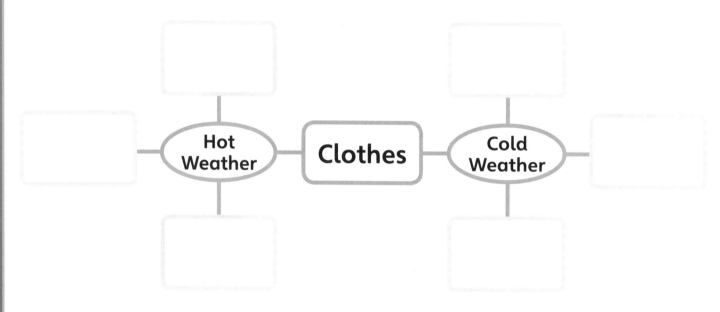

c l o t h e s   c o l d   j a c k e t

h o t   T - s h i r t   s h o e

1 Key Words 2 **Circle.**

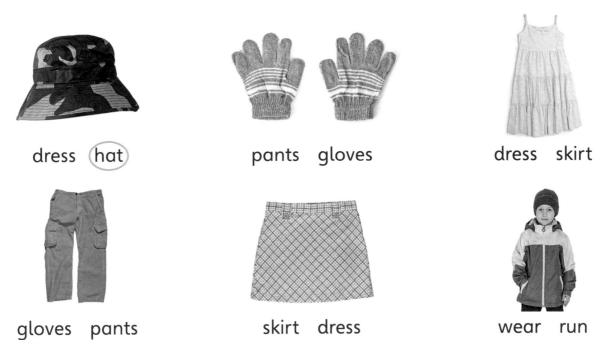

dress (hat)

pants   gloves

dress   skirt

gloves   pants

skirt   dress

wear   run

2 **Number. Trace. Color.**

____ pants

__1__ hat

____ skirt

____ dress

____ gloves

1

2

3

4

5

3 **Trace.**

I **wear** a hat. I wear gloves.

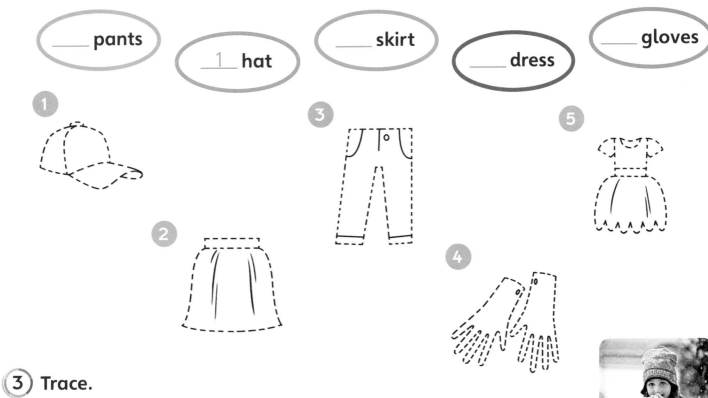

Reading Strategy: Cause and Effect

1 **Match.**

2 **Read** with your teacher's help.

Clothes

I'm Anaya. I'm from India. It's very hot here. It can be 40 °C!

I wear a sari and sandals. A sari is a long dress.

This is my favorite sari. It's blue. It's made of silk.

My name is Viktor. I'm from Russia. It's very cold here. It can be –40 °C!

When it's cold, I wear gloves, a warm jacket, and boots.
I love playing in the snow!

3 **Match.**

It's hot. She wears sandals.

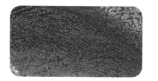

This is her favorite sari.

It's cold. He wears gloves.

His jacket is warm.

He wears boots.

4 **Match.**

sandals

40 °C   **cold**

Russia

hot

India

boots   **-40 °C**

Present Continuous: Affirmative and Negative

I'm wearing **a jacket.**
I'm not wearing **a T-shirt.**

She's wearing **a jacket.**
She's not wearing **a dress.**

(1) Match.

a I'm wearing a skirt.

b He's wearing gloves.

c I'm wearing a T-shirt.

d She's not wearing gloves.

(2) Circle.

She's wearing a skirt.   She's not wearing a skirt.

He's wearing a hat.   He's not wearing a hat.

(3) Trace.

I'm wearing pants.

I'm not wearing a hat.

4 Color.

I'm
I'm not
wearing gloves.

He's
He's not
wearing a jacket.

He's
He's not
wearing shoes.

I'm
I'm not
wearing pants.

5 Write.

He's   He isn't   She's   She isn't

_____ wearing a red dress.

_____ wearing a skirt.

_____ wearing a hat.

_____ wearing a jacket.

My Life

What are you wearing? Mark ✓.

① **Say. Circle.**

We play in Grandma's garden.

We see two green plants in Grandma's garden.

We eat the plums from the plants in Grandma's garden.

② **Trace. Number.**

1 green

2 plant

3 grow

4 plum

③ **Write gr or pl.**

p l a n t   _ _ o w   _ _ a n d m a   _ _ u m

① **Trace.**

These are my favorite clothes.
This is my favorite jacket. It's blue.

Questions

A question begins with a **capital letter** and has a **?** at the end.
How old are you? Do you like T-shirts?

1 **Circle.**

Find the questions.

What's your favorite jacket?

I'm wearing a T-shirt.

Do you like these red gloves?

What color is your hat?

It's cold!

How old are you?

2 **Mark ✓ the questions.**

How old are you? ☐

What's your favorite color? ☐

This is my jacket. ☐

Do you like it? ☐

I'm six. ☐

It's blue. ☐

What color is it? ☐

Yes! ☐

3 **Trace. Match.**

Is it cold?   It's orange.

What are you wearing?   No, it's not. It's hot.

Do you like it?   Yes, I can. Let's go!

What color is it?   I'm wearing a T-shirt.

Can you play?   Yes! I love it!

4 Trace.

What's your name?

How old are you?

Is it hot?

What are you wearing?

What's your favorite color?

5 Write . or ?.

What's your name ___

What's your favorite color ___

How old are you? ___

My name is Eva ___

It's blue ___

I'm six ___

1 Key Words 4 **Circle.**

(emperor) thief

smart   expensive

clothes   palace

smart   fool

2 **Trace. Match.**

palace

expensive

emperor

thief

Reading Strategy: Beginning, Middle, and End

1 **Number 1, 2, and 3.**

1
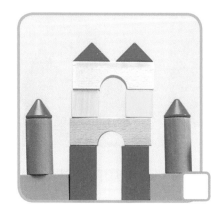

2 **Read** with your teacher's help.

The Emperor and the Thief

Emperor, I love your shoes!

Look at the emperor's shoes!
They are very expensive.

He's not wearing his shoes!
He's a fool! I'm smart!

The emperor is sleeping in the
palace. A thief sees the shoes!

Oh, no!
The shoes
aren't real!
I'm mad!

The thief is in the forest.
It's raining. Look at the shoes!

The thief is
a fool! Here
are the real
shoes!

The emperor is smart.
He has the real shoes.

3 Number.

4 Match.

1 Oh, no! The shoes   the real shoes!

2 The emperor is   a fool!

3 The thief is   smart.

4 Here are   aren't real.

5 Match.

not real shoes   **real shoes**

thief   **fool**

emperor   **smart**

Grammar in Context

Present Continuous: *Yes/No Questions*

Are **you** wearing **pants?**
Are **you** wearing **a skirt?**

Yes, I am.

No, I'm not.

1 Circle.

Are you wearing a jacket?

Are you wearing a hat?

Are you wearing gloves?

Are you wearing pants?

Yes, I am. /
No, I'm not.

Yes, I am. /
No, I'm not.

Yes, I am. /
No, I'm not.

Yes, I am. /
No, I'm not.

2 Match.

you / Are / pants / wearing / ?

shoes / wearing / you / Are / ?

you / Are / a jacket / wearing / ?

a hat / wearing / you / Are / ?

Are you wearing a jacket?

Are you wearing shoes?

Are you wearing a hat?

Are you wearing pants?

3 Trace.

Are you wearing gloves ? No, I'm not.
Are you wearing a skirt ? Yes, I am.

(4) **Complete.**

Are you	I am	I'm not

Are you wearing pants? Yes, _I am_ .

_____ wearing gloves? No, _____ .

_____ wearing a jacket? Yes, _____ .

(5) **Trace and write the questions.**

1

_____ Are you _____
wearing a dress ?

2

_____
_____ ?

> **My Life**

What are your favorite clothes? Draw.

1 How can you take care of your clothes? Mark ✓.

2 Match.

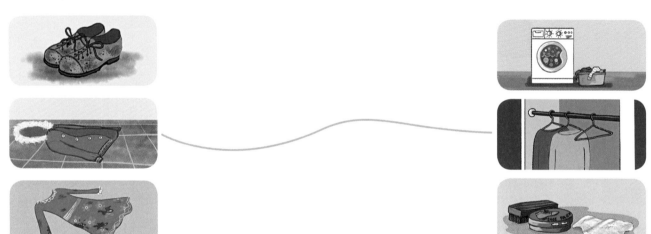

3 How do you take care of your clothes? Draw.

I wash my clothes.

176

The Big Challenge and Oracy

How do we dress for special occasions?

Answer with your teacher's help.

Color 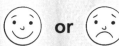 or .

1 I talked about clothes we wear for special occasions.   **or**

2 I made a jigsaw puzzle.   **or**

3 I described what the person is wearing.   **or**

Oracy

Check Your Oracy!

1 I presented to my group.	**Yes / No**
2 I stood still.	**Yes / No**
3 I stood up straight.	**Yes / No**

At school, I wear ...

1 Circle. Match.

f	g	h	c	s	w	c	o
d	o	g	l	o	v	e	s
r	g	r	o	t	g	t	k
p	a	n	t	s	a	h	i
e	l	s	h	a	t	e	r
s	k	t	e	h	c	r	t
d	r	e	s	s	l	m	v

2 Color.

2 jackets   6 shoes   4 T-shirts   3 gloves

3 Trace.

w o o l hat

c o o l weather

9

4 **Circle.**

He's wearing a hat.   I'm wearing a dress.   She's wearing a skirt.
He's not wearing a hat.   I'm not wearing a dress.   She's not wearing a skirt.

I'm wearing a jacket.   I'm wearing gloves.
I'm not wearing a jacket.   I'm not wearing gloves.

5 **What are you wearing? Trace. Color.**

Are you wearing shoes?

Yes, I am.
No, I'm not.

Are you wearing a dress?

Yes, I am.
No, I'm not.

Are you wearing a hat?

Yes, I am.
No, I'm not.

6 **Circle.**

She's wearing a skirt.

Are you wearing a jacket?

Look at that shoe!

I like that T-shirt.

Do you like this hat?

What is your favorite color?

1 **Circle.**

school   toys   home   animals

routines   clothes   food

2 **Match.**

Please ———— understand.
I don't ———— repeat that.
Good   you!
Thank   job!

3 **Match.**

This is my drawing.

Please repeat that.

Thank you.

Good job!

What can you remember about ... Unit 9?

1 Color.

I'm wearing
I'm not wearing
a dress.

2 Match.

She's wearing a hat.

He's wearing a hat.

3 Circle.

Are you wearing gloves?

Yes, I am.

No, I'm not.

4 Mark ✓.

shoe ☐
skirt ☐

5 Circle the question.

How old are you?   I'm six.

6 Trace.

gr_een_   pl_ant_

7 Circle.

Two / Three thieves go to the palace.

8 Circle.
hot
cold

Check your answers in the Student's Book. How did you do?
6–8 ☐ Great!   3–5 ☐ Good!   0–2 ☐ Try harder!

? 😀 **Why do we wear different clothes?**

Circle.   It's cold.

It's my birthday party.

It's hot.

It's expensive.

All About Oracy!

Unit 1: Ground Rules

1 This is …

Unit 2: Agreeing and Disagreeing

School is fun! Do you agree?

Yes!

No!

2 Yes.

3 No.

Unit 3: Active Listening

4 Please repeat that.

Unit 4: Taking Turns

Let's play. I'll start.

It's my turn. Now it's your turn.

5 It's my turn.

6 It's your turn.

Unit 5: Participating Actively

7 Let's …

Unit 6: Asking for Agreement

8 Do you agree?

2 Yes.

3 No.

Unit 7: Giving and Responding to Positive Feedback

9 Good job!

10 Thank you.

Unit 8: Speaking Up

11 I don't understand.

4 Please repeat that.

Unit 9: Standing Up Straight and Keeping Still during Presentations

12 These are …

1 This is …

Acknowledgments

The authors and publishers acknowledge the following sources of copyright material and are grateful for the permissions granted. While every effort has been made, it has not always been possible to identify the sources of all the material used or to trace all copyright holders. If any omissions are brought to our notice, we will be happy to include the appropriate acknowledgments on reprinting and in the next update to the digital edition, as applicable.

Key: U = Unit.

Photography

The following photos are sourced from Getty Images.

U1: Jose Luis Pelaez Inc/DigitalVision; BlackJack3D/iStock/Getty Images Plus; Leontura/DigitalVision Vectors; liangpv/DigitalVision Vectors; David Freund/Photodisc; binik/iStock/Getty Images Plus; Greig Reid/Moment; Hero Images; Moof/Cultura; RichLegg/E+; Katerina Sisperova/iStock/Getty Images Plus; Amy Lockard/E+; Rudy Poupin/EyeEm; Emma Kim/Cultura; Layland Masuda/Moment; saiyood/iStock/Getty Images Plus; Ismailciydem/iStock/Getty Images Plus; Sally Anscombe/DigitalVision; JBryson/iStock/Getty Images Plus; Elke Van de Velde/Photodisc; SensorSpot/E+; ideabug/E+; Flashpop/DigitalVision; Daniel MacDonald/dmacphoto.com/Moment; Andersen Ross Photography Inc/DigitalVision; Roberto Westbrook/Image Source; Rubberball/Erik Isakson; Anna Pekunova/Moment Open; JW LTD/DigitalVision; Paperboat/E+; pinstock/E+; Jon Boyes/Tahreer Photography/Moment; iSci/E+; burakpekakcan/E+; Tom And Steve/Photographer's Choice RF; ChristopherBernard/E+; KathyDewar/iStock/Getty Images Plus; shumelki/E+; lostinbids/iStock/Getty Images Plus; drbimages/E+; primeimages/iStock/Getty Images Plus; The India Today Group; zahoor salmi/Moment; Annika H./500px Prime; Dave & Les Jacobs/DigitalVision; Janie Airey/Cultura; Paul Bradbury/Caiaimage; Maskot; kali9/E+; Chris Upson/Moment; Teddi Yaeger Photography/Moment; Esthermm/Moment Open; Jack Hollingsworth/Photodisc; JGalione/E+; Morsa Images/DigitalVision; REB Images; andresr/E+; Lyn Walkerden Photography/Moment; SolStock/E+; Clover No.7 Photography/Moment; Trevor Williams/DigitalVision; PeopleImages/E+; Weeraya Siankulpatanakij/EyeEm; Image Source; Johner Images/Brand X Pictures; Andrea Ricordi, Italy/Moment; alvarez/E+; Zolotaosen/iStock/Getty Images Plus; Tanya Constantine; PeopleImages/iStock/Getty Images Plus; Anastasiia_M/iStock/Getty Images Plus; Nick Dolding/The Image Bank; eli_asenova/iStock/Getty Images Plus; Westend61; emholk/E+; Ed Bock/Corbis; Imagesbybarbara/iStock/Getty Images Plus; Emely/Cultura; Imagesbybarbara/E+; ArtMarie/E+; Fotosearch; Dave_Pot/iStock/Getty Images Plus; Destinations by DES - Desislava Panteva Photography/Moment; Bombaert Patrick; Mohd Haniff Abas/EyeEm; Ivan/Moment; Sally Anscombe/Taxi; RyanJLane/E+; AYImages/E+; Philippe Gelot/Photographer's Choice; hardik pethani/iStock/Getty Images Plus; U2: manonallard/E+; Longmongdoosi/iStock/Getty Images Plus; ChiccoDodiFC/iStock/Getty Images Plus; kali9/E+; monkeybusinessimages/iStock/Getty Images Plus; constantinopris/iStock/Getty Images Plus; fotolism_thai/iStock/Getty Images Plus; Jupiterimages/Stockbyte; wakila/E+; DGLimages/iStock/Getty Images Plus; Image by J. Parsons/Moment; Rick Gayle/Corbis; Aping Vision/STS/DigitalVision; Siede Preis/Photodisc; Ziva_K/E+; malerapaso/iStock/Getty Images Plus; Mosutatsu/E+; Samohin/iStock/Getty Images Plus; ArisSu/iStock/Getty Images Plus; dlerick/iStock/Getty Images Plus; MirageC/Moment; clubfoto/iStock/Getty Images Plus; Marc Espolet Copyright/Moment; Jean-Marc PAYET/Moment Open; big_Ryan/DigitalVision Vectors; Tatabrada/iStock/Getty Images Plus; eli_asenova/iStock/Getty Images Plus; gerenme/E+; FatCamera/E+; EyeMark/Stock; Getty Images Plus; spaxiax/iStock/Getty Images Plus; hatman12/iStock/Getty Images Plus; Boger Anna/EyeEm; Hemera Technologies/PhotoObjects.net; annebaek/iStock/Getty Images Plus; 992/Moment; Leonardo Carneiro Photographic Art/Moment; Ljupco/iStock/Getty Images Plus; kosmos111/iStock/Getty Images Plus; tiridifilm/E+; hudiemm/E+; Horned_Rat/DigitalVision Vectors; NYS444/iStock/Getty Images Plus; duckycards/E+; PeopleImages/iStock/Getty Images Plus; leolintang/iStock/Getty Images Plus; michaeljung/iStock/Getty Images Plus; kcline/E+; CRG STUDIOS; Nicole S. Young/iStock/Getty Images Plus; NoSystem images/E+; sarahwolfephotography/Moment; Image Source/Stockbyte; Tatiana Kolesnikova/Moment; PhotoAlto/Eric Audras/PhotoAlto Agency RF Collections; Westend61; Peter Muller/Cultura; Deborah Pendell/Moment; Jose Luis Pelaez Inc/DigitalVision; Light Bulb Works/Moment; Roberto Pangiarella/EyeEm; Hill Street Studios/DigitalVision; Arletta Cwalina/EyeEm; Jamie Grill; iammotos/iStock/Getty Images Plus; racnus/iStock/Getty Images Plus; Moussa81/iStock/Getty Images Plus; Fuse/Corbis; JGI/Jamie Grill; wsfurlan/iStock/Getty Images Plus; jaroon/E+; Stella; Alan Graf/Cultura; Jonathan Kirn/Photodisc; DNY59/E+; malerapaso/E+; Floortje/E+; stockcam/E+; skodonnell/E+; AYImages/E+; NNehring/E+; Stockbyte; northlightimages/E+; mphillips007/iStock/Getty Images Plus; Michael Zwahlen/EyeEm; Bulgac/E+; I2MN/iStock/Getty Images Plus; Ron and Patty Thomas/E+; selimaksan/E+; Kryssia Campos/Moment; Marffta/iStock/Getty Images Plus; U3: CGinspiration/E+; Stockbyte; Aslan Alphan/E+; iconeer/DigitalVision Vectors; stockcam/E+; Jose Luis Pelaez Inc/DigitalVision; Donald Iain Smith/Moment; Victoria J Baxter/Moment; Martin Barraud/OJO Images; ERphotographer/iStock/Getty Images Plus; MartenBG/E+; Don Farrall/Photographer's Choice RF; arsa35/iStock/Getty Images Plus; MediaProduction/E+; Jasmin Merdan/Moment; EasyBuy4u/E+; Lawrence Manning/Corbis; View Stock; wundervisuals/E+; Lane Oatey; Judith Haeusler/Cultura; Digital Vision/Photodisc; Nadia Swindell Photography/Moment Open; Marc Espolet Copyright/Moment; Ruediger Hirt/EyeEm; talevr/iStock/Getty Images Plus; lvcandy/DigitalVision Vectors; Theerasak Tammachuen/EyeEm; Sezeryadigar/iStock/Getty Images Plus; TongRo Images Inc; JGI/Tom Grill; Tim Hall/Cultura; H Jones/Cultura; Edgardo Contreras/Photodisc; Juanmonino/iStock/Getty Images Plus; Biddiboo/Photographer's Choice/Getty Images Plus; Motortion/iStock/Getty Images Plus; BLOOM image; Blue_Cutler/E+; Ariel Skelley/DigitalVision; BJI/Blue Jean Images; Rubberball/Erik Isakson; Natthawut Nungsanguansri/EyeEm; Elena_Ozornina/iStock/Getty Images Plus; Tomekbudujedomek/Moment; Life On White/Photodisc; Francesco Malorgio/EyeEm; JGI/Jamie Grill; Guerilla; Katrina Wittkamp/DigitalVision; Image Source/Photodisc; gerenme/E+; FatCamera/E+; alexsl/iStock/Getty Images Plus; leolintang/iStock/Getty Images Plus; Tony Garcia/Image Source; aphrodite74/E+; ZargonDesign/iStock/Getty Images Plus; Creative Crop/Photodisc; CSA Images; CTRPhotos/iStock Editorial; Hemera Technologies/PhotoObjects.net; Images by Christina Kilgour/Moment; Lezh/E+; paul mansfield photography/Moment; Jonathan Gelber; SDI Productions/E+; Didier Robcis/The Image Bank/Getty Images Plus; Christopher Hopefitch/DigitalVision; Fuse/Corbis; Alistair Berg/DigitalVision; JoeLena/iStock/Getty Images Plus; Garry518/iStock/Getty Images Plus; duckycards/E+; akinshin/iStock/Getty Images Plus; golovorez/E+; Suchart Doyemah/EyeEm; Susanna Price; skynesher/E+; Morsa Images/DigitalVision; Ian Nolan/Image Source; Westend61; Lane Oatey/Blue Jean Images; kali9/E+; Suwit Nimjitt/EyeEm; volschenkh/E+; Becart/E+; AndrewJohnson/E+; bbtomas/iStock/Getty Images Plus; skodonnell/E+; Michael H/DigitalVision; akud/iStock/Getty Images Plus; Soud Aldayoli/EyeEm; AnthonyRosenberg/iStock/Getty Images Plus; Echo/Juice Images; U4: skeeg/DigitalVision Vectors; IP Galanternik D.U./E+; clubfoto/E+; d3sign/Moment; Stella Kalinina; gerenme/E+; Carlina Teteris/Moment; Caiaimage/Charlie Dean; Charlie Dean/Caiaimage; Hero Images; Klaus Vedfelt/DigitalVision; Jasmin Merdan/Moment; Sandra Clegg/Moment; Christopher Hopefitch/DigitalVision; Carlos G. Lopez/Moment; Creative Crop/DigitalVision; deepblue4you/E+; Serghei Starus/EyeEm; Lya_Cattel/E+; Sisoje/E+; DigiStu/E+; Onzeg/E+; Per Magnus Persson; gerenme/E+; Stockbyte; Jacek Kadaj/Moment; Pakorn Kumruen/EyeEm; JBryson/iStock/Getty Images Plus; Andy Crawford; Jose Luis Pelaez Inc/DigitalVision; Alex Levine/500px; Jack Vance/500px/500Px Unreleased Plus; Click&Boo/Moment; marg99ar/iStock/Getty Images Plus; ivanastar/iStock/Getty Images Plus; Catherine Delahaye/DigitalVision; Heide Benser/Corbis; Tom Werner/DigitalVision; Phathn Sakdi Skul Phanthu/EyeEm; ozenli/E+; lostinbids/iStock/Getty Images Plus; Westend61; Christoph Hetzmannseder/Moment; Massimiliano Clari/EyeEm; jhorrocks/E+; adventtr/iStock/Getty Images Plus; pepifoto/E+; Juanmonino/iStock/Getty Images Plus; Birgit Korber/EyeEm; Nickilford/E+; Birgit R/EyeEm; Antagain/E+; Pablo Dolsan/EyeEm; Kwanchai Lerttanapunyaporn/EyeEm; Digital Zoo/Photodisc; Pierre-Yves Babelon/Moment; Jui-Chi Chan/iStock/Getty Images Plus; 35007/E+; Kulik Krisztin/EyeEm; Dagmar Schelske/EyeEm; Teddi Yaeger Photography/Moment; Gabriele Grassl/iStock/Getty Images Plus; TongRo Images Inc; Katrin Sauerwein/EyeEm; Benjamin Torode/Moment Open; Benedetta Barbanti/EyeEm; Stefka Pavlova/Moment Open; BFG Images; monkeybusinessimages/iStock/Getty Images Plus; SolStock/E+; Blend Images - JGI/Jamie Grill; Tetra Images; Csondy/E+; SelectStock/Vetta; JGI/Jamie Grill; fstopl23/E+; soleg/iStock/Getty Images Plus; ClaudioVentrella/iStock/Getty Images Plus; A. Chederros/ONOKY; mediaphotos/E+; Layland Masuda/Moment; Alan Tunnicliffe Photography/Moment; mawielobob/iStock/Getty Images Plus; Chee Siong Teh/EyeEm; skodonnell/E+; Ng Sok Lian/EyeEm; Jureeporn Chaiyapram/EyeEm; CRG STUDIOS; Oliver Dexter/EyeEm; mikroman6/Moment; Daniel Grill; photograpy is a play with light/Moment; U5: Akepong Srichaichana/EyeEm; Stephanie Zieber/iStock/Getty Images Plus; Maria Toutoudaki/Stockbyte; DaveThomasNZ/E+; Christian Hacker; Benedetta Barbanti/EyeEm; Robert Kneschke/EyeEm; Lucinda Lee/EyeEm; Elisa Cappelletti/EyeEm; huronphoto/E+; Vera Shestak/iStock/Getty Images Plus; fototrav/E+; Photo by Bill Birtwhistle/Moment; Rachel Collings/EyeEm; Eric Middelkoop/EyeEm; David Tipling/DigitalVision; Buck Shreck/500px Prime; vojce/iStock/Getty Images Plus; morgan stephenson/Moment; Nick Brundle Photography/Moment; joegolby/iStock/Getty Images Plus; Westend61 - Gerald Nowak/Brand X Pictures; Stockbyte; gemredding/iStock/Getty Images Plus; Volga2012/iStock/Getty Images Plus; chengyuzheng/iStock/Getty Images Plus; Robert Lang Photography/Moment; Dimitris66/iStock/Getty Images Plus; angintaravichian/iStock/Getty Images Plus; ikonacolor/iStock/Getty Images Plus; cheri3l/iStock/Getty Images Plus; Westend61; Sue Barr/Image Source; BJI/Blue Jean Images; Gary Chalker/Moment; Alex Tihonovs/EyeEm; Marko Konig; Fuse/Corbis; Alan Tunnicliffe

Photography/Moment; Sophie Hermbusche/EyeEm; DeepDesertPhoto/RooM; Allan Baxter/Photodisc; Mark Kostich/E+; Jose A. Bernat Bacete/Moment; Xuanyu Han/Moment; Todd Aki/Moment Open; seng chye teo/Moment; Anup Shah/DigitalVision; David Lazar/Moment; Fei Yang/Moment; sekarb/iStock/Getty Images Plus; Fernando Trabanco Fotografia/Moment; Pierre-Yves Babelon/Moment; Barbara Fischer, Australia./Moment; Photos by R A Kearton/Moment; Posnov/Moment; Funwithfood/E+; irakite/iStock/Getty Images Plus; Saddako/iStock/Getty Images Plus; Martin Priestley/Moment; Jenny Rainbow/EyeEm; Michael Runkel/Moment; Jacky Parker Photography/Moment; Arun Roisri/Moment; dibrova/iStock/Getty Images Plus; Carol Yepes/Moment Open; Panak Sriwantana/EyeEm; Enrique Ramos López/EyeEm; Amir Mukhtar/Moment; jopstock/Moment; Gordon Ogletree/EyeEm; Fleetham Dave/Perspectives; Wanida Saetung/EyeEm; Photography by Jeremy Villasis. Philippines./Moment Open; Steve Gorton/Dorling Kindersley; onurdongel/E+; malerapaso/E+; Devonyu/iStock/Getty Images Plus; Rubberball/Erik Isakson; MirageC/Moment; Eshma/iStock/Getty Images Plus; turk_stock_photographer/iStock/Getty Images Plus; James Neno/EyeEm; Jeff Greenough; Sergio Alcarazo/EyeEm; Stuart Westmorland/Stockbyte; Terry Lawrence/EyeEm; 4045/iStock/Getty Images Plus; mangpor_2004/iStock/Getty Images Plus; U6: Ariel Skelley/Photodisc; Annie Otzen/Moment; Caiaimage/Paul Bradbury/OJO+; Weekend Images Inc./E+; 2A Images; skynesher/E+; Imgorthand/E+; by Ibai Acevedo/Moment; Chip Simons/Stockbyte; NPHOTOS/Moment Open; BJI/Blue Jean Images; shumelki/E+; Funwithfood/E+; Johner Images; Isabella Antonelli/EyeEm; cjmckendry/E+; Jessica Peterson; FatCamera/E+; Marilyn Nieves/E+; TongRo Images Inc; Welcome to buy my photos/Moment; Elizabethsalleebauer/RooM; JGI/Jamie Grill; Radius Images; Katja Kircher/Maskot; View Stock; Photo and Co/Stockbyte; susan.k./Moment; Gary S Chapman/Photographer's Choice RF; rbv/iStock/Getty Images Plus; Paul Barton/Corbis; Allen Donikowski/Moment; ImagesBazaar; timsa/E+; CareyHope/E+; Núria Talavera/Moment Open; FGorgun/E+; C Squared Studios/Photodisc; Jose Luis Pelaez Inc/DigitalVision; Kinzie Riehm/Image Source; Thai Yuan Lim/EyeEm; Jure Gasparic/EyeEm; Maica/E+; Tanya Constantine; Photodisc; George Doyle/Stockbyte; Dean Mitchell/E+; Lane Oatey/Blue Jean Images; huronphoto/E+; CsarsaGuru/E+; boschettophotography/E+; fatihhoca/E+; PetrBonek/iStock/Getty Images Plus; Jupiterimages/Polka Dot; Caiaimage/Robert Daly/OJO+; PBNJ Productions; phollapat cheechang/iStock/Getty Images Plus; Ableimages/DigitalVision; Tetra Images/DigitalVision; Nick Ridley/Oxford Scientific; Martin Deja/Moment; Elles Rijsdijk/EyeEm; SrdicPhoto/E+; princessdlaf/E+; Maartje van Caspel/E+; Fuse/Corbis; jaroon/E+; Sasiistock/iStock/Getty Images Plus; Milkos/iStock/Getty Images Plus; Dallin Willden/EyeEm; kohei_hara/E+; Geber86/E+; monkeybusinessimages/iStock/Getty Images Plus; Photograph taken by Alan Hopps/Moment; Deborah Pendell/Moment Open; QuimGranell/Moment; chengyuzheng/iStock/Getty Images Plus; Dorling Kindersley; macida/E+; ozgurdonmaz/iStock/Getty Images Plus; Hero Images; Ben Bloom/DigitalVision; Jutta Klee; Bob Langrish/Dorling Kindersley; ViewStock; Rob Lewine; Peter Cunningham/EyeEm; Westend61; Beo88/iStock/Getty Images Plus; kali9/E+; Ivan Olianto/Moment; annebaek/E+; Carolyn Ann Ryan/Moment; Victoria Bee Photography/Moment Open; mustafagull/E+; IvanJekic/E+; Image Source; Teresa Short/Moment; Ghislain & Marie David de Lossy/Cultura; RiniSlok/iStock/Getty Images Plus; Andrea Colarieti/EyeEm; Jostein Nilsen/EyeEm; Paula Daniëlse/Moment; Tim Hall/Cultura; Cavan Images; Petri Oeschger/Moment; Tatiana Kolesnikova/Moment; Image Source; mfto/DigitalVision Vectors; U7: Rastko Belic/EyeEm; Ryoji Yoshimoto/Aflo; jerryhat/E+; Gerhard Schulz/Photographer's Choice; YinYang/iStock/Getty Images Plus; EasyBuy4u/E+; Alter_photo/iStock/Getty Images Plus; I09508Liane Riss; strizhakov/iStock/Getty Images Plus; Doable; tanuha2001/iStock/Getty Images Plus; dlerick/iStock/Getty Images Plus; Nattawut Lakjit/EyeEm; Pinghur Chen/EyeEm; clubfoto/iStock/Getty Images Plus; mbbirdy/E+; Artur Szczybylo/EyeEm; kedsanee/E+; Atw Photography/Photolibrary; robynmac/iStock/Getty Images Plus; asbe/iStock/Getty Images Plus; LOVE_LIFE/E+; kertlis/iStock/Getty Images Plus; Kativ/iStock/Getty Images Plus; drewhadley/E+; Sergey Ivanychev/EyeEm; Maximilian Stock Ltd./Photolibrary; Blue Images/Corbis; Joel Brouwer/Moment Open; Simon_Taplin; AndreyCherkasov/iStock/Getty Images Plus; Jose Luis Pelaez Inc/DigitalVision; LauriPatterson/E+; harmpeti/iStock/Getty Images Plus; Okea/iStock/Getty Images Plus; waiwai08/iStock/Getty Images Plus; gavran333/iStock/Getty Images Plus; Yothin Sanchai/EyeEm; MahirAtes/iStock/Getty Images Plus; Magone/iStock/Getty Images Plus; UpperCut Images; JGI/Jamie Grill; Westend61; Corbis/VCG; Roberto Machado Noa/LightRocket; PauloVilela; Yevgen Romanenko/Moment; xxmmxx/iStock/Getty Images Plus; Natthawut Nungsanthern/EyeEm; Mizina/iStock/Getty Images Plus; JBryson/iStock/Getty Images Plus; A-S-L/iStock/Getty Images Plus; monticello/iStock/Getty Images Plus; dcdr/E+; DNY59/E+; ma-k/E+; Nathalie Salman/EyeEm; Schaefl/iStock/Getty Images Plus; Tarik Kizilkaya/E+; Emmanuelle Bonzami/EyeEm; Life On White/Photodisc; Yutthana Teerakarunkar/EyeEm; Blend Images - Todd Wright; Rubberball/Mike Kemp; niphon/iStock/Getty Images Plus; Mint Images - Norah Levine/Mint Images RF; Marco Livolsi/EyeEm; CaseyGrillPhoto/E+; Melanie Hobson/EyeEm; gerenme/E+; Kunal Sehrawat/EyeEm; republica/E+; pjohnson1/E+; Aleaimage/E+; milanfoto/E+; Birgit R/EyeEm; tovflc/E+; Thomas Firak Photography/Photolibrary; Robert Daly/OJO Images; Martin Brigdale/Dorling Kindersley; DarrenMower/E+; Gary John Norman/Cultura; RichVintage/E+; PacoRomero/E+; ozgurdonmaz/iStock/Getty Images Plus; esseffe/E+; cmannphoto/E+; pixelfit/E+; BOMBAERT Patrick; Creativ Studio Heinemann; Sian Irvine/Dorling Kindersley; Wladimir Bulgar/Science Photo Library; subjug/iStock/Getty Images Plus; yalcinsonat1/iStock/Getty Images Plus; marilyna/iStock/Getty Images Plus; CareyHope/E+; Arx0nt/iStock/Getty Images Plus; 5PH/iStock/Getty Images Plus; Martin Deja/Moment; Natthakan Jommanee/EyeEm; AlasdairJames/E+; Acharaporn Kamornboonyarush/EyeEm; Chris Ted/Stockbyte; DawnPoland/E+; 4X-image/E+; Oliver Helbig/EyeEm; Stuart Minzey/Photographer's Choice RF; Juanmonino/E+; Classen Rafael/EyeEm; gaffera/E+; Chee Siong Teh/EyeEm; Herbert Kratky; DonNichols/E+; hardik pethani/iStock/Getty Images Plus; U8: Tetra Images; Ariel Skelley/DigitalVision; Jose Luis Pelaez Inc/DigitalVision; Caiaimage/Robert DalyCaiaimage; kali9/E+; Westend61; Hero Images; HKPNC/E+; Indeed; Peathegee Inc; Nick David/DigitalVision; ferrantraite/E+; Alexander Spatari/Moment; photobody/iStock/Getty Images Plus; ImagesBazaar/Brand X Pictures; zia_shusha/iStock/Getty Images Plus; ugurhan/E+; onebluelight/E+; Kittiphan Teerawattanakul/EyeEm; nmaxfield/E+; Amit and Naroop/Image Source; PeopleImages/E+; James Osmond/Photolibrary; Imgorthand/E+; vitapix/iStock/Getty Images Plus; Westend61/E+; SolStock/E+; BJI/Blue Jean Images; wsphotos/iStock/Getty Images Plus; 2011 Dorann Weber/Moment Open; Image Source; Blend Images - JGI/Jamie Grill; ChristopherBernard/E+; FatCamera/E+; Getty Images Plus; jorgeantonio/iStock/Getty Images Plus; Enn Li Photography/Moment Open; Martin Harvey; imagimina/E+; arlindo71/E+; Ryan McVay/Photodisc; PLAINVIEW/E+; PhotographerOlympus/E+; Tomwang112/iStock/Getty Images Plus; imagenavi; Lane Oatey/Blue Jean Images; 3sbworld/iStock/Getty Images Plus; photosindia; JGI; vesi_127/Moment; Richard Cummins/Lonely Planet Images; With love of photography/Moment; leezsnow/iStock/Getty Images Plus; ARO @ PHOTOGRAPHY/Moment Open; Elizabethsalleebauer/RooM; Stephan Hoeck; Comstock/Stockbyte; Julien de Wilde/ONOKY; Caiaimage/Robert Daly; pinstock/iStock/Getty Images Plus; Jamie Grill/The Image Bank/Getty Images Plus; Sasato Krungsee/iStock/Getty Images Plus; Mlenny/E+; Pollyana Ventura/E+; TongRo Images Inc; moodboard/Cultura; Sally Anscombe/DigitalVision; Monsterstock1/iStock/Getty Images Plus; Photodisc; Visage/Stockbyte; ktaylorg/E+; huronphoto/E+; JohnnyGreig/E+; kostins/iStock/Getty Images Plus; Adam Heste/Stockbyte; David De Lossy/Photodisc; Weekend Images Inc./E+; Gallo Images (Pty) Ltd; Rubberball/Mike Kemp; Clover No.7 Photography/Moment; YouraPechkin/iStock/Getty Images Plus; Science Photo Library phototropic/E+; Cavan Images; eliflamra/iStock/Getty Images Plus; sensationaldesign/iStock/Getty Images Plus; U9: Bill Diodato/DigitalVision; Volker Schlichting/EyeEm; BJI/Blue Jean Images; SergiyN/iStock/Getty Images Plus; DNY59/E+; Ng Sok Lian/EyeEm; Yevgen Romanenko/Moment; Stockbyte; Sawitree Pamee/EyeEm; Jitalia17/E+; Howard Shooter; Scott Suriano/Moment Open; triloks/E+; MRaust/iStock/Getty Images Plus; Vladimir Godnik; NattyHongPhoto/iStock/Getty Images Plus; photo_stella/iStock/Getty Images Plus; Hemera Technologies/PhotoObjects.net; DonNichols/E+; OcusFocus/iStock/Getty Images Plus; sam74100/iStock/Getty Images Plus; 3sbworld/iStock/Getty Images Plus; dcdebs/E+; Lane Oatey/Blue Jean Images; Imagesbybarbara/E+; Digital Vision/Photodisc; Sean Sequeira/Moment; hide/iStock/Getty Images Plus; Andy Crawford/Dorling Kindersley; Aliaksandr Bahdanovich/iStock/Getty Images Plus; avtk/iStock/Getty Images Plus; Chee Siong Teh/EyeEm; R.Tsubin/Moment; LockieCurrie/E+; c_bell/iStock/Getty Images Plus; malerapaso/E+; ranasu/E+; Jacob Wackerhausen/E+; Stuart Minzey/Photographer's Choice RF; Y.Nakajima/un/ANYONE/amana images; Image Source/Photodisc; VikramRaghuvanshi/E+; hartcreations/iStock/Getty Images Plus; Jose Luis Pelaez Inc/DigitalVision; wakila/E+; Photodisc; Tarzhanova/iStock/Getty Images Plus; Nirut Punshiri/EyeEm; Yellow Dog Productions/Photodisc; C Squared Studios/Photodisc; Adél Békefi/Moment; vasiliki/E+; Piotr Polaczyk/iStock/Getty Images Plus; dendong/E+; JoKMedia/E+; Dorling Kindersley; bobtphoto/E+; ideabug/E+; Comstock/Stockbyte; Klaus Mellenthin; izusek/E+; abejon/E+; a-clip; Rebecca Nelson/Moment; JGI/Jamie Grill; Pimmas Duangmee/EyeEm; Rubberball/Chris Alvanas; Isabel Pavia/Moment Open; huronphoto/E+; Jessica Holden Photography/Moment Open; severija/iStock/Getty Images Plus; levente bodo/Moment.

The following photo is sourced from another source.

U8: Courtesy of European Commission.

Illustrations

Illustrations by Adriana Quezada; Benedetta Capriotti; Dave Williams; David Shephard; Dean Gray; Denise Hughes; Dragan Korvic; Hannah Wood; James Hearne; Leo Trinidad; Lesley Danson; Lisa Hunt; Lucy Semple; Melanie Demmer; Morgan Huff.

Cover illustrations by Bao Luu (Astound).